D1301261

DATE DUE

GAYLORD			PRINTED IN U.S.A.

Adlai: The Springfield Years

Adlai: The Springfield Years

By
Patricia Harris

AURORA PUBLISHERS, INC.
NASHVILLE/LONDON

WITHDRAWN
OESTERLE LIBRARY
CORE COLLEGE
NAPERVILLE, ILLINOIS 60566

COPYRIGHT © 1975 BY
AURORA PUBLISHERS, INCORPORATED
NASHVILLE, TENNESSEE 37203
LIBRARY OF CONGRESS CATALOG CARD NUMBER: 73-76522
STANDARD BOOK NUMBER: 87695-167-1
MANUFACTURED IN THE UNITED STATES OF AMERICA

973.921
St 4
H24a

For Dick
and
Barbara Anne

Contents

Introduction

His face distorted by the graininess of the television set, his voice strained with open emotion, the stocky, rumpled-looking, balding man on the screen startled Americans watching the United Nations proceedings throughout the country.

Glaring with unaccustomed ferocity at the Russian delegate to the United Nations and president of the Security Council, Ambassador Valerian Zorin, the man demanded:

"Do you, Ambassador Zorin, deny that the USSR has placed and is placing medium and intermediate-range missiles and sites in Cuba? Yes or no? Don't wait for the translation! Yes or no?"

And Zorin's taken-aback reply — this man's belligerent manner was not in keeping with his customary pronounced courtesy:

"I am not in an American courtroom, sir, and therefore I do not wish to answer a question that is put to me in the fashion in which a prosecutor puts questions. In due course, sir, you will have your answer."

But his questioner persisted.

"You are in the courtroom of world opinion right now, and you can answer yes or no. You have denied that they exist and I want to know whether I have understood you correctly."

"Continue with your statement," Zorin floundered. "You will have your answer in due course."

"I am prepared to wait for my answer," came the retort, "until hell freezes over, if that's your decision!"

The year was 1962, on a Thursday, October 25, and for several days thereafter the news accounts portrayed Adlai Stevenson as the country's plain spoken hero who had bored straight through to the issue—a somewhat different portrait from the one painted by the media during the preceding years of an indecisive "Hamlet" who had difficulty making himself understood.

1

Watching him on television, I could never quite associate the Adlai Stevenson I knew with the United States Ambassador to the United Nations. Following his post-presidential campaign career in the news, only occasionally did I catch a flash of him which struck a note of remembrance—vivid and poignant—sometimes the whimsical tilt of his head captured in a newspaper photo or the sudden warmth of a joking remark on television. He had little about which to exude warmth in those darkening days.

Even from such a distance of space and time, it seemed to me that he was burning himself out. During that period of his life, he had so much to haunt him that I was not surprised to read about his long hours of work and his frenetic pace. The intensity of the man was fierce, the pressures on him cruel.

Of course, his second presidential campaign in 1955-56 (when I put in several nerve-shattering months in his press office in Chicago) had been a crashing disappointment—not so much, I believe, because of the results but because of the marked disposition of some of his staffers to use his campaign as a vehicle for personal gain.

Then, too, groping for a way in which to engage President Dwight Eisenhower in battle a second time without seeming to detract from his image as a hero was, perhaps, the most frustrating period of his life. This was mirrored graphically in a memorandum he wrote at that time to his staffers asking rather plaintively if anything was being done about combating propaganda.

From what I knew of the man, I found it quite in keeping with his character when he accepted the ambassadorial post in 1961 under President Kennedy. Stevenson was never a good spectator. He was too much a man of action to "sit in the shade with a glass of wine and watch people dance," as he was quoted by newsman Eric Sevareid as desiring just before his sudden death in London in 1965.

But the catastrophic Bay of Pigs invasion attempt and the explosive political aftermath in which he stood accused in a *Saturday Evening Post* "inside" article as an appeaser, his turbulent relationship with President Kennedy, who blithely left Stevenson holding the bag before the whole world, the merciless use of the man by those in power to whom integrity was a sometime thing—all this was an overpoweringly harsh finale to any man's life. And I believe he died before his time.

Threading through our friendship of some eighteen years, despite long gaps of silence, was the bond of our Springfield years together. We "grew up" there—a cub reporter and a new governor—in our respective worlds of news and government, which meshed for four fast-moving years in which I watched with fascination as he rose from an unknown Chicago lawyer-candidate to a world-famous presidential contender.

There was something distinctly disturbing about watching the metamorphosis. We left Springfield almost at the same time, when I resigned my news job to enter the field of public relations, and he went down to defeat for the first time in his presidential campaign. Thereafter, until I joined his second campaign, we exchanged letters now and then, and always the tone of our communications reflected the years before, as he put it, the "iron curtain" of fame had descended upon him.

Once when he was governor, he asked me after a news conference if I recalled offhand the source of a poem from which he quoted a line or two. It was Robert Frost's "Stopping by Woods on a Snowy Evening":

> "The woods are lovely, dark and deep,
> But I have promises to keep,
> And miles to go before I sleep,
> And miles to go before I sleep."*

Adlai Stevenson went those weary, troublesome miles but I believe that in his mind, he often returned to Springfield where it all began.

*From "Stopping By Woods on a Snowy Evening" from THE POETRY OF ROBERT FROST edited by Edward Connery Lathem. Copyright 1923, © 1969 by Holt, Rinehart and Winston, Inc. Copyright 1951 by Robert Frost. Reprinted by permission of Holt, Rinehart and Winston, Inc.

CHAPTER ONE

"The People Don't Like What They've Heard"

In the Springfield of 1948, Dwight Green was governor of Illinois; Dick Daley had not yet arrived as state senator (in fact, he had just been defeated as a candidate for sheriff in Chicago); and Adlai Stevenson was introduced to us in a room at the St. Nicholas Hotel.

At that time, there were three popular hangouts for the politicians who came down to Springfield from Chicago and needed a place to congregate where drinks were handy, a degree of privacy could be attained and it was possible to wander through a dining room which offered not only prime steaks but a chance to table-hop from contact to contact. They were the Abraham Lincoln Hotel (which the Republicans favored), the St. Nicholas Hotel (for the Democrats), and the Leland Hotel (a sort of meeting ground).

The Lincoln, a fading dowager, basking in worn-out opulence, boasted a tavern which was small, always crowded and offered green-tinted beer on St. Patrick's Day. This little mecca for elbow benders was, of course, not open to black citizens, a simple fact which seemed to bother nobody except a group of both black and white persons from Chicago who once entered the dining area to demand service. When they were thrown out, they marched down the street to sit under the statue of Abraham Lincoln in front of the statehouse and eat sandwiches.

An enterprising news photographer took a picture which went out on the wires all over the country and which surprised many residents of Springfield. They couldn't understand what was newsy about a bunch of "pinkos" and their black friends being tossed out of the American Room of the Abraham Lincoln Hotel!

5

A block away stood the old Leland Hotel, which was more informal in atmosphere and offered superb barroom facilities through the services of a man known to most of us as just "Matt the Bartender." Matt not only mixed strong drinks but also negotiated settlements when arguments erupted. It was said that he was the originator of a popular item on the menu called the "Horseshoe," which consisted of a wild combination of "mix and match" sliced ham, sliced chicken, fried eggs and French fries with a beer-cheese sauce over all. Downed after a brace of Matt's martinis, it was magnificent!

The St. Nicholas Hotel was somewhat out of the political swim, being located several blocks away from the heart of downtown Springfield but nonetheless a pleasant old edifice with a respectably interesting Revel Room bar off the lobby. The press conference which had been called for Adlai Stevenson took place in a small room upstairs and was what his supporters chose to call a "simple" affair. Or, in other words, cheap. No drinks, no snacks. The Republicans, who had all the money that year and most of the offices, introduced even the lowliest of their candidates with the best bonded bourbon and shrimp hors d'oeuvres, but the Democrats weren't about to throw around what little they had on a man who wasn't going to win anyhow.

Stevenson's introduction to the Springfield press was more in the nature of a formality than anything to get excited about. All three major news services were represented—Associated Press, United Press and International News Service (of which I was local bureau manager) but our questions were perfunctory and polite. We actually knew very little about the man and the paths that had led him to this Springfield hotel room where he stood nervously answering questions in an atmosphere of forced joviality.

Reportedly, Secretary of State James Byrnes had mentioned Stevenson's name to Chicago Democratic leader Jacob M. Arvey at an informal luncheon in Washington the preceding year. However, Byrnes had suggested Stevenson for a position as United States Attorney in Illinois.

Arvey was on the lookout for two candidates—one for

governor and one for U.S. senator and when he returned to Chicago he called Judge Harry M. Fisher, who was a friend of Stevenson's. Shortly after, Fisher got Arvey and Stevenson together.

Some time later, a Chicago lawyer named Lou Kohn heard Stevenson speak at a meeting of the Chicago Council on Foreign Relations and went to work with two other men to set up a "Stevenson for Senator Committee." The other two were Hermon Dunlap Smith and Stephen Mitchell. According to the Chicago newspapers, these three prevailed upon Arvey to "discover" Stevenson. The catch, however, was that Arvey had Paul Douglas in mind, but after several weeks of worrying the matter around, Stevenson agreed to go for governor. Recommendation by a kingpin like Arvey was, of course, tantamount to nomination in the Democratic primary.

Douglas, a University of Chicago economics professor, was a former Marine who had been wounded at Okinawa. Arvey was well aware of the fact that the incumbent Republican Senator, C. Wayland "Curley" Brooks, ran largely on his World War I record and his possession of the Croix de Guerre, and he felt correctly that Douglas was the ideal candidate to pit against him. And quite frankly, nobody expected to beat Gov. Dwight Green. Stevenson was really given an assignment that nobody wanted, and the only advantage was that he wasn't expected to accomplish anything other than rack up some practical political experience.

Running with Stevenson were Sherwood Dixon for lieutenant governor, Edward J. Barrett for reelection as secretary of state, Ivan Elliott as attorney general, Benjamin O. Cooper as auditor, and Ora Smith as treasurer. Eddie Barrett was the only real political pro on the ticket and the only one who would go on running for and holding elective office in various capacities until 1973 when he would run afoul of the law (as they like to put it) for income tax evasion.

Eddie was the oddball on the amateur ticket—not only because of his professional standing but because of his propensity for emulating his idol, Dick Daley, in mangling the English language. He once told us that he would have "photosphats" of his speeches made for us, and when somebody countered acidly that the interest in them was negligible, he replied innocently:

"Thank you. I think so, too."

All we had been told about Stevenson from his news release was that he was forty-eight years old, a Chicago lawyer and a recently appointed alternate delegate to the United Nations who had had some sort of government experience in Washington. As I shook hands with him, I felt sorry for him. He was up against too much.

Aside from the fleeting impression that he was painfully eager and had a high voice, I wasn't particularly impressed. Nor were any of the other reporters present. We were all more interested in the latest addition to Stevenson's campaign staff (we never did figure out his title), a forty-four-year-old giant of a man named Louis Ruppel, who had battled his way years ago from a job as stenographer in the meter department of New York's Consolidated Edison into journalism with such gusto that he had propelled himself right out onto the street again. He had started his news career in 1924 as a reporter for the *New York American* and four years later worked for the *New York Journal*. When he was twenty-six he became a political writer for the *New York Daily News,* a job he held until 1933 when he became U.S. Deputy Commissioner of Narcotics in Washington, D.C. Two years later, at the seasoned old age of thirty-two, he was made managing editor of the *Chicago Times.*

In 1939, Ruppel joined CBS as publicity director for two years, then became assistant to the president of Crowell-Collier Publishing Company. He was forty-two when he moved into the extremely high powered job of executive editor of William Randolph Hearst's *Chicago Herald-American,* a position which was fleeting and explosive.

Although I didn't know it until later, Ruppel had just been hired by Stevenson at the rate of $1,200 a month. In a letter to Ruppel, Stevenson had specified that payment would be made "if, as and when the money becomes available by contributions and without any first priority." This was just $200 a month more than the rate paid Jim Mulroy, former managing editor of the *Chicago Sun,* which had merged with the

Chicago Times, leaving Jim without a job. Jim had told me some time earlier that after the merger, he had been recommended to Stevenson by publisher Marshall Field. Nobody would ever admit knowing who had recommended Ruppel.

I had first met Lou at a party at the governor's mansion in 1945 when he was in his $40,000 a year job with the *Chicago Herald-American.* He was the last of the "Front Page" editors—unfortunately too late to qualify for full membership in that renowned group of gaudy newsmen who roared around city rooms trying to act like Walter Howey. Had Ruppel been born a few years earlier, his talents would have been appreciated more. As it was, he hit the newspaper scene at about the time the "yellow" in journalism was fading into a dull gray.

Although he was a graduate of New York's battleground, he was Chicagoese right down to his toes. When he was managing editor of the *Chicago Times,* he had one of his reporters committed to a mental hospital as a patient and bannered the story "SEVEN DAYS IN THE MADHOUSE." From what I had heard, his reporter had found those seven days peaceful compared with the *Times* city room. Ruppel was not noted for tact, gentle persuasion or all-round geniality.

When World War II interrupted his slam-bang career, he served his time as a Marine captain, then raced back into Chicago to the *Herald-American* editorship. We all knew he hadn't lasted long there. William Randolph Hearst, it was said, had bought out his contract and Ruppel had dropped from sight. That is, until that day at the St. Nicholas Hotel when he stood with Adlai Stevenson at the press conference. They were an incongruous pair.

"You still working in that little news bureau?" Ruppel bellowed at me with his customary tact, while Stevenson winced.

I told him I had just been promoted to manager.

"Well," he said, "stick around and when this is over, I may buy you a drink."

Later, over our bourbon at the Revel Room downstairs, he asked me what I'd heard about him.

9

I knew he had rocked the city in early 1945 with a front page article in the *Herald-American* topped by a big banner line: "THIS IS THE STORY OF OUR DIRTY SHIRT TOWN!"

I also knew that he had run pages of copy and photos of slum areas depicting the most sordid living conditions, and that his campaign had lasted three weeks before Chicago's civic and business leaders, particularly those with real estate interests, had put the heat on Hearst to call off his editor. Ed Kelly, who was then mayor, had protested to Hearst personally that Ruppel was slamming a stigma on the city with the "Dirty Shirt" title.

There was a strong rumor that the slumlords had threatened to pull out their advertising from the *Herald-American* if the series continued. At this point, Ruppel began running the names of the slum property owners in captions underneath some of the most wretched scenes. Hearst summoned Ruppel out to his San Simeon castle in California to "suggest" that the series be discontinued. When Ruppel returned to Chicago, he was met at the airport by a reporter from a news magazine.

"What happened?" the reporter asked.

"Oh," Ruppel replied laconically, "me and the old son-of-a-bitch talked it over and now I see things his way."

When the news magazine went to press a short time later, the editor had run Ruppel's reply with blanks in the appropriate places and Ruppel immediately received another invitation to San Simeon.

As I told Ruppel over our drink:

"I heard that Hearst fired you."

"Naw!" he rasped. "He bought out my contract."

What had taken place at "The Chief's" castle, I wanted to know.

"Aw," he growled, "nothing much. You oughta seen the dogs he had runnin' around all over the place—dogs, dogs, dogs—on account of Irene Castle being a friend of Marion Davies, you know."

"What did you do after you left the *Herald-American*?" I asked.

"Looked for a job. Got me a baby photo studio going. I've

come up in the world. Now I'm a chauffeur for Adlai Stevenson!"

"You ought to be back in news work," I observed.

He shrugged.

"Well, baby," he said, "you have got to remember that the *New York Times* doesn't need me."

Then, with his customary abruptness, he launched into a diatribe against several Chicago newsmen who, he said, hated him with all their black little hearts and were glad to have seen him go. Seems he had once fired them. He couldn't understand why that made them mad.

"Why those sons of bitches!" he exploded. "When they saw me coming along the street in the Loop, they crossed to the other side!"

What about this man Stevenson, I asked him.

"Listen," he said, "he really thinks he's going to win and I'll tell you something. I think he can do it. Provided he listens to me, of course."

I mentioned that I wished somebody would do something about housing for the veterans who were back from the war and who had just picketed Governer Green at the mansion. Green had thoughtlessly signed a proclamation earlier for a humane association in which the words "a good home for every dog" were used. With much glee, a group of veterans contending with the post-World War II housing shortage, had marched around the mansion with signs reading: "GOOD HOMES FOR DOGS BUT NOTHING FOR VETERANS."

Ruppel was interested.

"Get me the name of that veterans' group and their address," he ordered. "I want them."

He seemed to feel that, since Hearst also owned International News Service, Ruppel was an honorary lifetime client by reason of his former association with the *Herald-American*.

Two or three weeks after our drink, I received the following letter from him on blue letterhead reading, "ALL-ILLINOIS STEVENSON-FOR-GOVERNOR COMMITTEE" at 7 South Dearborn Street in Chicago:

June 1, 1948
Dear Pat:

I will be up in northwestern Illinois for a while but that ain't what I am writing about, kiddo. Get me those veterans' names and stuff and ship them here so I will have them when I get back.

Sincerely,
Louis

On July 8, he wrote me again about it:

Dear Pat:

When you see the story you sent me all done over and in somebody's column, you will hardly recognize it.

Off to the convention Friday. Will call you when next in Springfield.

Sincerely,
LR

That was the last I heard from Lou Ruppel until 1950 when he was to run head-on into Adlai Stevenson with explosive results. As far as Stevenson's gubernatorial campaign was concerned, Ruppel was just out and nobody on the campaign had ever heard of him.

Dick Daley was a delegate to the Democratic National Convention in Philadelphia that year. Chicago's Mayor Martin Kennelly was a delegate-at-large. So were Sen. Scott Lucas and Col. Jack Arvey.* With all the furor over Harry Truman insisting on running, we didn't hear much about Stevenson.

Moreover, it was definitely a Republican year, what with Tom Dewey a cinch to beat Truman in the national race. Stevenson was just a token candidate in a token try, although I am certain his motive in running was not just to oblige the Democrats. He might have been reluctant to go for it at first, but once committed, he fought as if his survival depended on the outcome.

* Who used to be Jake Arvey until he asked the press to stop calling him that and to use "Jack" instead.

In the little town of Peru, he spoke—"I don't believe irresponsible promises are good politics. Promise-peddling and double-talk may be expedient and catch some votes from the unwary and innocent, but promises also have a way of coming home to roost."

When Governor Green condescendingly referred to Stevenson as a "cookie pusher" and a member of the "striped pants brigade," Stevenson shot back with:

"I have read Governor Green's speech when he opened the Republican campaign. He damns me with being on leave from the 'striped pants brigade to the Roosevelt-Truman State Department.' Damned or striped—I will keep my pants on!"

Green's condescension backfired. The *Chicago Daily News* printed a picture of him wearing striped pants, top hat, cutaway and white waistcoat—along with the notation that there was no photo in their files showing Stevenson similarly attired.

Green's ascension to the executive mansion four years earlier was an interesting matter. He had been an assistant U.S. attorney at the time of Al Capone's conviction for tax evasion and was credited with bringing this about. The people of Illinois had just seen the so-called sordid "100 days" following the death of Gov. Henry Horner and the seizure of the state government by the most disreputable type of politicos, who got away with almost everything but the dome of the statehouse. Voters wanted somebody like Dwight Green, who exuded an aura of honesty and capability and who, incidentally, had silver-gray hair, handsome (almost fatherly) features and a pleasant smile. He looked the way a governor should look!

And for a while he tried to ignore his cocky challenger. But Stevenson was punching harder and harder, and the blows were beginning to sting a little, although not to an alarming degree. One of his statements, which intrigued me so much that I kept a copy of an excerpt, was made early in the year before the Democratic State Central Committee:

"The crude, old-fashioned spoils politics of the state administration cannot be veiled forever by virtuous pronouncements. The people don't like what they've heard and they will like it less and less as they hear more and more about what's been done and what's not been done in the last eight years."

But interlaced with his serious pronouncements were the witticisms—the refreshingly bright humor which was so different from the customary corn doled out by Illinois' not-so-intelligent office seekers. At the time, nobody seemed to feel that his humor was a detriment to the campaign. Quite the opposite. A relative unknown, he was attracting attention and gathering a sympathetic audience. Moreover, he was punctuating his speeches with enough wit to keep the listeners awake and interested.

What was infinitely more fascinating to me was the "behind-the-scenes" action which evolved around three fortuitous events (fortuitous for Stevenson, of course—catastrophic for Green). One was the aftermath of a coal mine explosion in Centralia the preceding year, in which it was brought out that some of the mine owners had been contributing heavily to Green's campaign fund via solicitation by several of the state's mine inspectors. An inspector blew the whistle on them after the Centralia explosion, which resulted in the deaths of 111 miners, and a lengthy investigation followed. I covered some of the hearings, particularly those in which miniature explosions were touched off to demonstrate how easily this can be done in a mine. The result of the investigation did not place the blame on Green but scattered the responsibility by reporting that the mine companies, the miners and the unions had all been lax in inspections and in adherence to safety regulations. Still, the mine payoff aspect hurt Green's campaign considerably, and Stevenson was quick to take advantage of it in his speeches. In that year, downstate Illinois (heavily Republican) was saturated with coal mines and the issue was charged with all types of ramifications.

Stevenson's biggest break by far came when the Shelton case exploded. I was in my office on a sizzling July 26 when our correspondent in Peoria called me. A few minutes later,

I had 'broken" the teletype wire to Chicago and was sending out five bells and:

BULLETIN
Peoria, July 26—(INS)—Bernie Shelton died today with a slug in his chest and his lips sealed in gangland code.

The 50-year-old former member of a prohibition era gang was conscious for half an hour after he was rushed to St. Francis Hospital, but he refused to name the assassin who felled him with one bullet in front of the Parkway tavern.

-more-152PPM

I was much too busy handling the story to think of any possible ramifications at the time. Just a door away, three bright, energetic, ruthless United Press newsmen were working the story, too, and we always raced to beat each other to the wire with something good. (Associated Press down the hall in the city room of the *Illinois State Journal-Register* never offered us competition where speed was concerned— just more thorough coverage by dint of a larger staff).

No sooner had I polished off the last "add" than Chicago sent me a coded message that UP was carrying a "mysterious green car speeding from the scene of the crime."

Hastily, I called my correspondent back. No, he said, he knew nothing about a mysterious green car. In fact, he was positive there had been none, as he had been at the scene of the slaying and had interviewed eyewitnesses. I sent a message to Chicago to this effect. Back came another coded message that stated stubbornly that UP was going to get all the play from the editors with their mysterious green car. I got the point. I put an "add" onto my story about a mysterious BLUE car speeding from the scene of the crime and that gave the editors a chance to pick their favorite color.

Of course, even Stevenson had no idea at the time that the sudden death of a tough Peoria gangster would have an effect on a campaign unimaginatively launched as "The New Look in Illinois Politics." The first I knew of it came when the *St. Louis Post-Dispatch* began running a series of articles based on secret recordings which Bernie Shelton had made of his conversations with various highly placed state officials who were members of Governor Green's organization. It seems that Shelton had exercised some forethought by leaving instructions that in the event of his assassination, the recordings be forwarded intact to the *Post-Dispatch*. The contents were devastating to the Green administration in terms of wholesale corruption and bribery among some of his top lieutenants.

Although Green himself was not personally involved, he was hurt—and badly hurt—by the sensational revelations. Shelton was the brother of a southern Illinois gang leader named Carl, who had been assassinated earlier while free on $6,000 bond. Carl had been charged with assault with intent to kill as the result of a fist fight in front of the same tavern where Bernie had been shot down. Nine months before Bernie's death, Carl had been gunned down while driving a jeep near Fairfield, Illinois.

The *Post-Dispatch* sent reporter Ted Link to Peoria, where he uncovered evidence of ties between the gamblers and law officials. It was brought out from the recorded conversations that some of Green's people had been taking payoffs from gamblers, slot machine operators and the like.

Just to put the frosting on it all, the newspaper's Roy Harris and the *Chicago Daily News'* George Thiem, both stationed in Springfield, went to work together on a news tip that a number of Illinois newsmen were being carried on the state payroll in nonexistent capacities. When that little gem broke, I let our Chicago office handle it. I had a vision of our business chief in New York watching the wire with glazed eyes as we happily exposed the fraudulent activities of some of our most lucrative editor clients.

I was also more than a mite shocked over the involvement of newsmen in the whole messy business. They were all employed in various editorial capacities on small-town papers throughout downstate Illinois and, although I knew none of them personally, I felt that some of the mud had spattered on all of us in the profession.

Scandals like that didn't help us any where politicians were concerned. They tended to lump us all together—and, of course, we returned the favor! I knew that bribery and payoffs of various types went on, but I wasn't particularly happy that so many newsmen were caught up in it. The only thing that made me feel that we had a comeback was that the scandal had been uncovered by two of our own and not by a political candidate or special prosecutor.

It was a tragic affair, however, in terms of human wreckage. One of the newsmen who was fired as a result wandered into my office several days later to apply for a job—and to assure me that he wouldn't mind a bit working for a young girl. He was in his forties and had spent his entire career on the same small Illinois daily.

"They wouldn't give me a raise," he said, "but they told me they could put me on the state payroll. They said everybody did it that way. I've got a wife and four kids, so what the hell?"

Sure, I thought—what the hell? But why did the people over him, who had suggested the deal, get home free?

At any rate, the scandals all gave Stevenson a huge boost and he made the most of it. Still, the Democratic party's publicity campaign manager, Spike Hennessey, told me that they had raised less than $100,000 for their campaign instead of the $250,000 they had hoped for, while the Green machine had at least five times that much to play around with.

"Hell," Spike said glumly, "we don't even have a speech writer. Stevenson writes his own stuff."

The stuff must have been pretty good. At the time of the Democratic National Convention in Philadelphia, the betting odds were 10 to 1 against Stevenson. By election night in November, the odds had dropped to 5 to 1 but Stevenson was still listed by the bookies as a very long shot.

All election nights in newsrooms were mass confusion but particularly so in our case where all three news services were housed within spying distance on the same floor—an unusual arrangement. Associated Press outnumbered INS massively in personnel. During routine months, they employed a minimum of four to five persons in their Springfield bureau, including one or two teletype operators, while extra reporters were added to cover legislative sessions.

In the United Press office, a bureau manager covered more territory on a faster schedule with the help of two full-time reporters and a teletype operator.

My International News Service bureau ran under three employees—me, a full-time assistant and a teletype operator, plus one part-time reporter during the legislative sessions. Yet my territory included all of downstate Illinois from Peoria to an imaginary line just north of St. Louis, Missouri. And in all that area I listed only three regular correspondents—one each in Peoria, Champaign-Urbana and Quincy.

Things being what they were, I had no choice but to use my initiative, imagination and foresight. Or, in other words, to steal my news wherever I could and try not to get caught at it. I was selective about it. I stole prep basketball and football scores from United Press because they came in fastest in that bureau and their teletypes were in an outer office conveniently placed near the door where I could step up and read them quickly.

Associated Press machines, unfortunately, were past their main office and absolutely unapproachable without my being detected. However, they maintained an elaborate network of stringers and on election night were really unbeatable in thoroughness (if not in speed). Best of all for me, they always set up a big blackboard just outside their door in the city room of the *Journal-Register* and methodically chalked up the returns for all to see. It was easy for me to step into the hallway, jot down the latest and rush the figures by teletype to Chicago for relay on the trunk wire (coast-to-coast).

It worked beautifully—in fact, too beautifully. I was teletyping the figures so rapidly that I began beating Associated Press with their own statistics and they threatened to complain about me.

On election night in November of 1948, I was cautiously peeking down the hall at their blackboard when my office phone rang. A perplexed INS newsman in Chicago wanted to know what was going on down there. I didn't know what he meant.

"Are your figures right on Stevenson?" he asked me.

"So far as I know," I said. "Why?"

"Can you check out a few areas and let us know?" he asked. "There's something funny going on."

When I glanced at the wire, I knew why he was puzzled. The downstate figures I was sending up to him were totaled in the Chicago office with the figures from the remainder of the state, and the running total was indicating an unbelievable trend toward Stevenson. Hastily, I called a few sources. They confirmed the statistics. Not only was Stevenson taking Republican downstate, but he was headed towards a smashing victory.

To confuse the picture even more, Harry Truman was having a "seesaw" time of it trying to capture Illinois. Instead of getting away after midnight as I had expected, I was up all night in the bureau working returns and when it was all over, although Truman barely carried the state by 33,612 votes, Adlai Stevenson got 572,067—the largest number ever polled for a winning gubernatorial candidate in the history of Illinois. He carried 48 of 101 downstate counties, a hitherto impregnable Republican fortress.

It wasn't long after it became official that a moon-faced little Democratic state politician named Paul Powell,* who hailed from Vienna, Illinois (pronounced Vie-enna), whooped happily in front of the press that:

"The meat's a-cookin!!"

And when Adlai Stevenson gave his "farewell" speech to Democratic party workers in Chicago, in which he said he would always be indebted to them as he prepared to leave for Springfield, the same Powell shouted:

"Don't worry, Adlai! We'll be there!"

---

* This was also the same Powell who went on to become Illinois Secretary of State and who died in October of 1970 leaving a grand total of $850,000 in cash in his Springfield hotel room and several bank accounts—which only proved that he was thrifty.

19

CHAPTER TWO

"It's a Good Bill and It Should Oughta Pass!"

When I first covered an Illinois legislative session, I was astounded to hear a state senator announce loudly from the floor:

"The ground was froze and the little peasants were hovering on the grass."

He seemed perfectly sober. From what I could see on the calendar in front of me in the press box, the bill on which he was speaking had something to do with changing regulations for hunting pheasants. When he sat down, I heard the clerk of the senate hiss at the president pro tem:

"How did he vote?"

Back came the answer:

"Mark him 'present.' He's there—even if he isn't *all* there."

This gentleman, however, was at least taciturn, unlike the representative who kept us all in convulsions over a gas storage bill when he got into a long, serious discussion on the "rights of intimate domain."

If we had been asked, we would have admitted candidly that perhaps only a dozen or so of the legislators were even mentally qualified to conduct the affairs of the state of Illinois. Several were practically illiterate. Others were alcoholic, openly corrupt or immoral.

One rather slow-witted senator, who liked to refer to building up an "iniquity" in real estate, never understood why the entire senate exploded one day when he was in the midst of what he thought was an eloquent defense of an insurance bill.

"This man had worked all his life building up his little grocery store. He was a good, honest man. Then along came this explosion of unknown origin." He paused for effect.

"And when this poor man woke up, he found he had completely lost his little business!"

It took twenty minutes to restore order.

We sat in the press box flanking the speaker's stand in each house, looking down on the people's choices from all over the state—the oddest mixture of representation I had ever seen. Everything outside Chicago and Cook County was largely rural and considered "downstate," while the big blustering city beside Lake Michigan sent down its legislators representing special interests. In addition, a bevy of hand-picked men from Chicago made up what was called the "West Side Bloc," popularly termed the "political action arm of the Chicago syndicate." It was explained to me that they were the remnants of the old Capone gang.

One member of the Bloc, State Rep. James J. Adduci, enjoyed the dubious distinction of having been arrested eighteen times between 1920 and 1933—but never convicted. Adduci livened up the first session I covered by challenging one of the political columnists to "step down out of that press box with your fists up!" The columnist shouted back that he'd meet him outside the House chamber ready to do battle, whereupon Adduci retorted that he'd be waiting for him on the statehouse grounds outside. At this point, Chicago Tribune's George Tagge commented laconically:

"When they get as far as the Leland Tavern, I'll cover it."

They never made it past our press room on the third floor and the issue of who was a liar, or whatever it was that had angered Adduci, remained in abeyance. He never came around the pressroom, although we were favored with many other visitors in the form of legislators, lobbyists and hangers-on. The room constituted the official headquarters of our Illinois Legislative Correspondents Association, and was a comfortable, carpeted air-conditioned place in which to write our stories, keep two Western Union senders busy and sit around afterwards drinking and talking.

It was in these inspiring confines that Tagge, who was the Tribune's suavest representative, concocted his "Philosophus T. Crump" publicity campaign. Tagge, intrigued by the name of this low echelon Chicago politician, began a practice of trying to slip Philosophus into as many stories as possible and, as his copy went through a number of different copy editors, he had a happy time of it. Whenever the mayor announced some new program, Tagge would poll a couple of politicos on their opinions and then add a line that "Philosophus T. Crump said such and such." Or, if a civic leader made a statement about something—almost anything—Tagge would manage to work in the opinion of Philosophus T. Crump. All else failing, he would have Philosophus either declining comment or unreachable at the moment.

Things reached the point where the harassed copy editors carried on a running battle with Tagge trying to detect and delete Philosophus, who began to take his publicity seriously and to call the city desk with his unsolicited opinions.

Tagge's closest crony in the pressroom was John Dreiske, who initially wrote a column called "Mugwump" which infuriated politicians with his acid wit and caustic comments. As president of our Illinois Legislative Correspondents Association, Dreiske engineered my election as vice-president at a meeting in the Leland Tavern—on grounds that I was useful to the newsmen as an errand runner, telephone answerer and good, all-round enthralled listener when they sat around telling wild stories.

Dreiske was a thoroughly indoctrinated Chicagoan with an utter disdain for anything outside that city. A graduate of Northwestern University, he had worked for the *Chicago Tribune*, the old *Detroit Mirror*, the *Detroit Times* and the *Chicago Herald-Examiner* before joining the *Chicago Times*. He knew his business. In addition to his regular job, he also worked as an instructor in the Medill School of Journalism at Northwestern, and when I expressed my admiration for his many talents, he replied disdainfully:

"It's just a lot of bullshit."

A sophisticated man, he was completely wrapped up in his profession and could wither people with elaborate sarcasm if he thought they were crowding in on him. Under his smooth manner lurked an aggressiveness that often astonished people who mistook this characteristic for an even disposition. When aroused, Dreiske was about as mild as a wounded buffalo.

The third newsman of this triumvirate was old Charlie Wheeler, a white-thatched raconteur of ribald stories which were absolutely unprintable and should have been unrepeatable. Charlie, who was seventy-five and the political editor of the *Chicago Daily News,* liked to slouch around the press room telling rambling anecdotes about the old Chicago *Inter-Ocean* newspaper and his years covering Eamon De Valera and the Irish Revolution.

In addition to Tagge, the *Tribune* had Bob Howard to bolster its coverage of politics, and special writers were sent down for specific events. Dick Orr, who was farm editor, covered any legislation pertaining to agriculture and Tom Morrow picked up items for a political news column. Their travel editor, Hal Foust, covered anything he wanted to, inasmuch as travel encompassed a vast territory.

It was with an exceptionally fine show of initiative that Hal arranged an enjoyable little junket every year to the warmer climes of Florida at the start of Chicago's ghastly winters. He would return to Chicago on such a slow, leisurely route that by the time he hit the outskirts of the city the winter's snow had melted and spring was in the air. Hal had so much luck getting away with this trip that his admiring friends dubbed it "meeting spring." That is, until the year the newspaper's business office cracked down on expense accounts and Hal's trip was canceled.

One of his more imaginative friends in the city room responded to the news by leaving a note in Hal's typewriter one day:

> Dear Hal:
> Why aren't you meeting me this year?
> Spring

The *Tribune* men worked hard for their dollars, however, and we never felt that their life was a barrel of laughs under the watchful eye of old publisher Col. Robert R. McCormick. After McCormick died, one of the newsmen liked to relate the story about two of the *Tribune* men in a bar discussing the death of an editor who had passed on just two days after the Colonel's demise.

"It sure was unexpected," said one over his beer. "He wasn't even sick."

"Well," replied the other reporter reflectively, "when the Colonel calls 'em, by God they come!"

A less restrictive atmosphere prevailed at the Chicago *Sun-Times* whose city editor was a thirtyish Karin Walsh and whose tone was more informal. In addition to Dreiske covering the legislative sessions, they had a full-time newsman, Hub Logan, stationed in Springfield, whose stories sometimes appeared under the byline: "From our Springfield bureau."

The "bureau" consisted of Logan in a hotel room with a telephone, a typewriter and a supply of western novels which he loved. He was a tough talking Kentuckian with a law degree, extensive news experience, a disarming "country boy" style and a finely honed talent for goading politicians into getting so mad that they sometimes blurted out the truth.

Logan was extremely sentimental but not everybody understood this. Once when a newsman said he and his wife couldn't find a baby-sitter for their son so they could attend a movie, Logan went to the phone in a burst of generosity, called the man's wife and graciously told her:

"I'll sit with the little bastard."

He never did understand why she turned down his offer.

These newsmen, plus the constantly changing personnel of the Springfield wire service bureaus, made up the first press line-up which Adlai Stevenson faced, and he fouled up matters before he even took the oath of office. Tickets to his big inaugural ball at the State Armory building were sent to Chicago ward heelers, downstate politicians, campaign workers, a large number of Stevenson's socialite friends and several Chicago news editors. But many of the working newsmen and women were overlooked, myself included.

On the preceding evening, Stevenson and at least seventy faithful party members had arrived in Springfield, occupying the last two cars of the Abraham Lincoln streamliner from Chicago. Governor Green had sent his old 1939, seven-passenger Cadillac to the station to have them driven to the Abraham Lincoln Hotel, where a lobby full of people dutifully cheered the entourage.

The following day, Stevenson and his family drove through a cold drizzle to the ninety-three-year-old executive mansion where Green presented them with the keys. Then, in a cavalcade of thirty-eight cars with white-gloved state policemen buzzing around on motorcycles and soldiers marching in the rain, they all headed for the National Guard Armory, where Stevenson took the formal oath of office.

Stevenson's inaugural address, which was given at noon, included references to a world in which "barriers of time and space no longer isolate us" and reflected his background in national affairs more than the narrow world of one Midwestern state.

"What Illinois can and must do," he said, "is to make itself the strongest link in that mighty chain which we call the United States. We can set our house in order. We can hearten our countrymen; we can demonstrate for all to see that representative government is healthy, vigorous, enterprising; that representative government is the best government. We can show the world what a government consecrated to plain talk, hard work and prairie horse sense can do."

Did he write that himself? We all wondered. We were told that he did.

One of the writers from outside Illinois noted in his story that the new governor had confounded us with the word "proliferation" in his inaugural address, presumably because we Midwesterners were none too literate. This was a typically condescending Eastern press attitude, which we encountered frequently throughout Stevenson's term.

That night when the politicians and the Chicago society leaders crowded into the armory where Louis Armstrong and Guy Lombardo took turns playing, we reporters went

The governor-elect and his wife are escorted into the mansion in Springfield. In less than a year, they were divorced.

(Left to right) Gov. Dwight Green and his wife, Mabel, greet Mrs. Ellen Borden Stevenson and the governor-elect. Behind Stevenson is his brother-in-law, Ernest Ives.

out to the Lake Club, where things were quieter and more to our liking.

One of the nicer aspects of Springfield in those days was a respectable assortment of gathering places, some of which offered top entertainment direct from Chicago at Springfield prices. It was a drinking man's town. *Tribune* columnist Morrow cracked that it had to be because nobody could stand it sober.

It also was a small city of many taverns and historical landmarks, of much Lincolniana, of long bitter winters when new snow drifted over the old unthawed sculpture powdered with the everlasting black soot from Illinois coal, of humid, corn-growing summers, of Future Farmers of America at the State Fair, and of multi-million dollar state scandals.

Wide open gambling flourished. Punchboards were displayed prominently beside cash registers. Cashiers offered to roll the dice "double or nothing" with customers. Blackjack tables, roulette wheels and slot machines abounded. Everything was so out in the open that when I first arrived there, I thought that gambling was legal.

It also seemed to me that a law must have been passed years earlier prohibiting any type of civic progress, slum clearance or new construction on the grounds that somebody might destroy a building that Lincoln had once leaned against. In the downtown area, for example, the county courthouse was actually hoisted up in the air so that an entire new story could be added underneath, resulting in a peculiar-looking building with a new first floor and ancient musty top floors reeking of Lincolniana.

Banks displayed Lincoln documents in glass cases. Plaques about Lincoln had been erected all over the city. There was the Lincoln Hotel, of course, and a Lincoln Public Library. Lincoln's home had been restored and reopened as a tourist attraction. Lincoln's tomb stood outside the city limits. The village of Old Salem had been rebuilt so that it appeared as it had in Lincoln's day. Several miles away in an ages-old cemetery rested Anne Rutledge with a Lincolnian epitaph over her grave, surrounded by long dead "Jacobs" and "Rachels" and "Jeremiahs." A couple of blocks from the governor's mansion still lived the sister of poet Vachel Lindsay, who had referred to Springfield as his "city of discontent" and who had written that "Abraham Lincoln walks at midnight" on its streets.

Lincoln walked during the daytime, too, every February 12, when peculiarly acting men sporting beards and stovepipe hats and frock coats wandered around looking like Lincoln. Tom Morrow even wrote a column once about how he thought a moratorium ought to be declared on this practice, as more and more "Lincolns" were showing up every year and pretty soon there would be so many men going around looking like Lincoln that there would be nobody left to look like anybody else.

When I heard that Adlai Stevenson was an addict of Lincoln lore, I felt he would feel right at home in Springfield.

Stevenson's first news conference as governor came the morning after his inauguration. He was in high spirits, tossing out witticisms all over his office in the statehouse and obviously enjoying the period in which, as a novice, he knew he was not expected to do much of anything. This was the traditional "honeymoon with the press" period granted to all public officials during their opening weeks in office.

I enjoyed watching him perform. It was obvious that he had a natural tendency to ham it up. He was not a prepossessing figure. At the age of forty-nine, and somewhat on the dumpy side, he stood only five feet five and one half inches tall and was a trifle overweight. He had a hawkish nose and he spoke rapidly but precisely in a high, clipped voice with a Midwest undertone.

There was something of the old school of charm about him, the noblesse oblige showing, and when he interrupted himself occasionally to explain a fine point to me, even though I had not asked, I interpreted his attitude as condescending toward women. He also was capable of cutting down a news reporter with a stinging retort. Yet, I sensed that he really wanted to be liked—particularly by the press. And underneath the actor was a most uncommon personality. At that point, I could only guess as to whether he was a charming fraud or a man of integrity.

His first news conference was one of the few he held in the statehouse. Thereafter, almost all of them were held in his basement office in the dowdy old mansion a few blocks away. Having been built in 1856, the three-story white brick and stone building was pretty run down and gloomy looking. I disliked the place because I always suspected they had a mouse problem. But Stevenson liked it. Old things seemed to appeal to him just because they were old. There were some twenty-five or thirty rooms, all high ceilinged, all on the funereal side. The roof had gables and the windows were long and narrow. In the entrance hall was an ivory white curving stairway with a mahogany handrail.

Entertaining was done on the second floor, which boasted a drawing room, a so-called music room, a state dining room with white paneling, a smaller dining room and a tile floored sun porch, which Stevenson later converted into a library. The bedrooms were on the top floor.

It was in the basement that he set up his little cubbyhole workshop of offices, and it was here he held his news conferences seated at a desk pushed up against a long table in T-formation. The legislators, quick to note his preference for the mansion, openly accused him of thinking he was "too good" to associate with them.

When he optimistically unloaded on them an unrealistically ambitious legislative program, they gleefully aimed their heavy artillery at it and proceeded to blast it to pieces. It was a methodically planned fiasco on their part to humiliate the new governor, and a number of the leading Democrats played footsie under the table with the Republicans to help accomplish this.

The "cat bill" was a typical example, except that Stevenson turned it to his advantage later in a classic veto message.

A Chicago Democrat, Sen. Roland Libonati (who also was a West Side Bloc figure) joined two other senators in sponsoring the bill. Under the provisions, stray cats could be scooped up and turned over to police or "proper agencies." It provided further that traps, approved by the Society for the Prevention of Cruelty to Animals, could be used by property owners annoyed by trespassing felines. Attracting birds by food or other special lures and deliberately sending out a cat to get the birds thus attracted were punishable by a fine of between $10 and $100.

The bill actually was not new. Back in 1945, one of the legislators introduced the measure at the request of a little gray-haired woman from Chicago named Gertrude Charney, who identified herself as president of "Friends of the Birds, Inc." She appeared before one of the legislative committees in all seriousness, displaying charts and reeling off statistics on how many food-destroying insects were eaten by one bird in the course of one month. The legislators had listened, thanked her for coming, and killed the bill.

Libonati, a white-haired senator with a cherubic countenance and a gift for mangling the King's English with elegance, thought it would be funny to resurrect the bill for Stevenson's benefit. Whenever the subject came up on the floor, the legislators all had a chance to utter loud "meows," which struck them as the height of subtle humor.

When he vetoed the bill, Stevenson wrote:

"I cannot agree that it should be declared the public policy of Illinois that a cat visiting a neighbor's yard or crossing the highway is a public nuisance. It is in the nature of cats to do a certain amount of unescorted roaming. . . . We are all interested in protecting certain varieties of birds but I believe this legislation would further but little the worthy cause. . . .

"The problem of the cat versus the bird is as old as time. If we attempt to resolve it by legislation, who knows but what we may be called upon to take sides as well in the age-old problem of dog versus cat, bird versus bird, or even bird versus worm. In my opinion, the State of Illinois and its local governing bodies already have enough to do without trying to control feline delinquency. For these reasons, and not because I love birds the less or cats the more, I veto and withhold my approval."

We were delighted to receive this unique veto message in our news offices and made good use of it.

It was Senator Libonati who also introduced a bill calling for cuspidors in public buildings. One of Stevenson's friends,

Ed Day (who became U.S. Postmaster General under President Kennedy) sent the following poem to John Dreiske for publication in his column, which proved only that Ed was an aspiring writer:

> A bill has passed the Senate
> About which some are skeptical.
> It would give a legal mandate
> To a rather crude receptacle.
> For those among the public
> Who do not approve of this,
> We point out that good government
> Should not be hit or miss.
> We recommend approval
> For Libonati's legislation.
> We feel sure it will live up
> To our best expectoration.

As it was customary for the press to host the governor at every regular legislative session, we set up a dinner party early in the year for Stevenson and his wife at the Leland Hotel in one of the ballrooms. Ellen Stevenson did not come, but he arrived with a couple of friends and proceeded to surprise us with a "thank you" speech in which he recounted a pretty bawdy joke about a U.S. Marine. The newsmen were not too pleased by this as there is nobody more prudish than a newsman when somebody else tells a dirty joke in mixed company, but it may be that Stevenson had not noticed the few girls present.

The absence of his wife at the dinner party provoked additional comment on top of that caused by Ellen's frequent absences from the mansion. More and more, Stevenson's sister, Mrs. Elizabeth Ives, was assuming the role of hostess at official functions. One of Stevenson's aides kept assuring us that nothing was wrong and that Ellen definitely would be present at the traditional governor's party for the press. There *was* one little change in store in connection with that party, he said—the locale had been changed to a local hotel ballroom instead of the executive mansion.

"By the Great Lord Jehoshaphat and all the saints in heaven!" exploded old Charlie Wheeler, who liked to talk this way. "If he thinks we're not good enough for the mansion, he can take his party and shove it!"

Just why Stevenson was planning to keep us out of the mansion was never made clear. There was absolutely no reason to move the party to a hotel, other than what we suspected—that he apparently considered us a drunken gang of uncouth slobs who would drop cigarettes on the carpeting, spill drinks on the furniture and, in general, cause no end of trouble. Perhaps he had been told of the all-night parties at the mansion under his predecessor and had jumped to conclusions that they were brawls. Actually, the only time I recall anything untoward happening was one night when a husky young reporter had too much to drink and belted another man halfway across the state dining room. His victim picked himself up, took careful aim and knocked his assailant flat. Then a state policeman came in and carted the limp newsman out and the party resumed. Other than that, the mansion galas were pretty prosaic, pleasant affairs featuring unlimited food and liquor and lasting as long as anybody cared to stay.

It bothered me that Stevenson did not want us, but it bothered me even more to realize that the newsmen were not going to show up at his hotel party. I had a vision of his pacing the floor, glancing at his watch periodically and seeing huge mounds of cracked ice melt, sending cold shrimp slithering to the floor while a big cut of roast beef* grew cold and a couple of bartenders stood silently behind a table of glasses and bourbon and Scotch watching Adlai Stevenson wait for guests that weren't going to show up. It made me think of the funeral of Fitzgerald's "Gatsby" when nobody came. Only Gatsby was dead and didn't know it, and Stevenson was very much alive. Somebody had to warn him.

Back in my office, I picked up the phone and dialed the mansion number.

---

* Which shows how little I knew about Adlai Stevenson then, as he usually served meat loaf with tomato sauce when he had his way about the menu.

CHAPTER THREE

And In This Corner— the Gentleman From Libertyville

Stevenson's appearance on the political scene had caught all of us by surprise. Almost before we could comprehend it, Dwight Green's old guard politicians were out, and the executive mansion was inhabited by a man about whom we really knew very little.

Time and again we referred to him in our news accounts as a political unknown whose rise in politics had been meteoric. Yet, his family background was so highly political, his interests so varied and his personality so extroverted that the real surprise was not that he was in politics but that he openly entered the field so late in life!

As I came to know him during that first year, he struck me as being intensely people-oriented and not at all the withdrawn, meditative type so often associated with people of extraordinary intellect. All of the years which had led him to Springfield were brimming with varied activity and experience.

In the year he was born in Los Angeles, his grandfather (for whom he was named) was the Democratic running mate of William Jennings Bryan in a campaign in which he failed to succeed himself as vice president of the United States. Adlai Stevenson, I, also ran for governor of Illinois in 1908 at the age of seventy-three, losing by 23,000 votes which was a respectable showing in a Republican year. Helen Davis Stevenson, who was Adlai II's mother, was the granddaughter of Jesse Fell, one of the founders of the Republican party and the man who suggested the famed Lincoln-Douglas debates. Fell also was one of the first to propose his friend, Lincoln, for the presidency.

33

Adlai's father, Lewis Green Stevenson, served as Adlai I's private secretary in Washington, D.C., where he met Mrs. Phoebe Hearst, widow of the mining millionaire, Sen. George Hearst. And this was the contact which started a chain of events leading ultimately to Adlai's intermittent entry into the world of journalism, his second love next to politics.

Adlai's father got a job as a newspaper correspondent and went to the Far East to report on the Sino-Japanese War. Upon his return, Lewis Stevenson was hired by Mrs. Hearst to help manage her mining properties in Arizona and New Mexico. After moving to Los Angeles, he was given a job by Mrs. Hearst's son, William Randolph—that of assistant general manager of the *Los Angeles Examiner*.

Adlai's interest in writing cropped up early in his life, and during the years I knew him, he mentioned often how much he would like to devote more time to writing. I believe this interest of his was the basis for his insistence later on in trying to write many of his own speeches during presidential campaigns.

Under different circumstances, it is possible that he would have become a full-time professional writer, but I think he had two handicaps—a gregarious personality, which made it difficult for him to spend much time alone, and enough money to keep the financial monkey off his back.

Stevenson's family always had money. When they left Los Angeles in 1906, they established a home in Bloomington surrounded by relatives, their roots deep in family tradition. They bought a two-story, gray stucco house, which still stands, and lived the life of the affluent, Adlai's father managing thousands of acres of crop lands and his mother handling the social life and the details involved in traveling between Bloomington and various summer and winter residences.

The Stevenson men apparently felt free to wander off in pursuit of the project of the moment, and Adlai was no exception. He was just eleven years old when he made his first trip to Europe, and he kept on traveling periodically through adolescence, young manhood and middle age.

34

He was not much of a scholar from the day he entered school at Winter Park, Florida, possibly because of his family's propensity for shuttling him and his sister around. He was transferred to the Bloomington public schools in the second grade but several years later his father was appointed to fill the unfinished term of an Illinois secretary of state who had died, and the family moved temporarily to Springfield.

When Adlai was sixteen, his father took him to Chicago to sit in on the Republican National Convention—the year Woodrow Wilson was after his second term, and the Republicans chose Charles Evans Hughes to run against him. So Adlai's interest in politics was based on an unusually high degree of personal involvement as a boy, and our frequent references to him as an amateur were, in fact, misleading. When he was graduated from Princeton, he was voted eighteenth most likely to succeed in a class of 325, but third biggest politician on campus.

From time to time, politics and writing cropped up throughout his younger years. He was twenty-four years old when he dropped out of Harvard Law School, went to work on the family newspaper, the *Bloomington Pantagraph*, and served as an assistant sergeant at arms at the Democratic National Convention in New York where he heard Franklin Delano Roosevelt speak for the nomination of Al Smith.

After a year as managing editor of the *Pantagraph*, he left to get his law degree at Northwestern University in Chicago and immediately used his father's contacts with the Hearst publishing empire to get hold of press credentials for a junket to Russia to interview Foreign Minister Georgi Chicherin. Adlai never succeeded in getting the interview, but he liked to reminisce about the adventure.

When he was married at twenty-eight (his bride, Ellen, was nineteen), he settled down for the first time in his life—for about five years. He worked as a law clerk for Cutting, Moore and Sidley, embarked on a social life and fathered three sons, Adlai III, Borden, and John Fell. And that was about as settled down as he was ever to get.

From there on, he worked in a variety of government jobs, commuting between Chicago and Washington on leave from the law firm. He served as a lawyer on the new Agricultural Adjustment Administration and as assistant general counsel for the Alcohol Control Administration in the wake of the repeal of prohibition.

He returned to Chicago, became one of eleven partners of the law firm, and at the age of thirty-six was named finance director for the Democratic National Committee in Chicago and state chairman of the Council of Roosevelt Electors. Next he became president of the Chicago Council on Foreign Relations and chairman of the Chicago branch of the Committee to Defend America by Aiding the Allies.

When he was forty-one, Adlai took a temporary job as special personal assistant to Secretary of the Navy Frank Knox, and then was appointed a special assistant to Secretary of State Edward R. Stettinius, Jr. He worked for the State Department on setting up the United Nations Conference that year in San Francisco and was honored with the Navy's highest Distinguished Civilian Service Award.

He and Ellen had bought a home in Libertyville near Chicago, but when he found time to visit there during all these years of running around was a mystery.

He worked again for Stettinius, who had been named chief American delegate to the Executive Committee of the Preparatory Commission of the United Nations, a job which necessitated moving his family to London to a small house just off Grosvenor Square. He also was named senior adviser to the United States delegation at the first meeting of the United Nations General Assembly on January 10, 1946, at Central Hall in Westminster. (Among the American delegates was Mrs. Eleanor Roosevelt.)

After returning to Libertyville, Adlai was in public service briefly as an alternate delegate at sessions of the United Nations in New York. And it was at this point that some of his friends began eyeing him as a possible candidate for the United States Senate.

His background, therefore, was hardly that of a provincial Chicago society lawyer with no political ties and only the foggiest notion of the problems entailed in running for office. He was not truly an amateur. He was more accurately a pretty seasoned "behind-the-scenes" worker in government, fascinated by the machinations of politics as against what he considered the deadly boredom of corporation law.

His trials and tribulations with his first session of the Illinois General Assembly stemmed from his lack of personal contact with the legislators. Although he seemed to grasp the implications of their nettling maneuvers before long, he was surrounded by staff advisers who were grossly inexperienced in politics. The result was comical. Stevenson gave the appearance of Lord Fauntleroy trying to convince the town bullies that they should toss away their brass knuckles and take up tiddlywinks. He committed the classic error of most new governors—a refusal to recognize the wants (and power) of the legislators and to bargain with them on this basis. He had only one aide on his staff, ex-newsman Jim Mulroy from his campaign, who at least understood that it was a tough world inside those legislative chambers and that you went to the inhabitants, hat in hand. But even Jim got tangled up along the way.

It took Stevenson a long time to distinguish between compromise and lack of integrity, but it was this very stubborn characteristic of his which appealed so strongly to the people. This was the Adlai Stevenson who would be disparaged later by his critics as a Hamlet on grounds that he was indecisive. The only vacillation I ever detected in the man during that first year as governor was his agony over spending money. Like most persons born into wealth, he wouldn't part with a nickel unless it was a national crisis. It always annoyed John Dreiske, who covered him during a great deal of his campaign, that Stevenson never got around to paying back the dimes and quarters he borrowed regularly—and John was too proud to ask. (We were quick to point out to John that this was why Adlai was wealthy and John was not.)

As most newly elected officials embark immediately on ambitious programs of economy, it attracted little attention when Stevenson went around during his first few weeks turning off lights in the unused rooms of the mansion. I decided he was really overdoing it when I noticed that he had had the little flags on his state limousine tied together to keep them from flapping in the breeze.

"They don't wear out as fast this way," he told me proudly.

At our first press party, which was held at the mansion after my telephone call to him, he set a pattern for future social gatherings which appalled us—two drinks, dinner, one brandy and then back out the front door fast. His idea of livening up that doleful party was to have us all line up while a photographer perched on the stairway and took a group picture. Somebody speculated that we had set a record for being the soberest guests at the mansion in a decade.

Stevenson's wife, Ellen, appeared briefly, mingled with us for a few minutes and then retired with a sick headache. I never saw her again.

As time went on, we learned that Stevenson had nothing against drinking except that it was expensive. Also, I suspect it went against his very nature when a person lost control of himself in public. I never saw him lose his temper publicly, but there were times when he was plainly angry and didn't hesitate to voice his feelings. Instead of roaring at people, he froze, and he did it effectively enough to freeze them right out of the room when he wanted to.

Whatever he considered petty in humans irritated him. After one news conference during that first legislative session, *Chicago Tribune's* Johnson Kanady stayed to tip him off that two rather highly placed state officials were feuding to the point of confrontation. Johnson, who had assumed that Stevenson would thank him and then mediate the matter later, was perfectly astonished to be told peevishly:

"I can't concern myself with the trivial affairs of those people."

A few weeks later, one of the officials walked up to the other official in the statehouse coffee bar and knocked him cold. But, as Johnson told us disgustedly when the story ran on the front pages, he would bet that Stevenson still didn't give a damn. And elsewhere in the statehouse, the carnage continued.

Stevenson's main legislative proposal, a constitutional convention resolution, was killed in the House almost before the session was well under way. A state fair employment practices bill which he had endorsed staggered through the House only to fall under the Senate axe on a close vote. FEPC was beaten by a 23 to 25 vote on June 16 after almost three hours of blistering floor debate. A solid wall of Republicans, joined by one Democrat, rang up the 25-vote tally. Six Republicans joined seventeen Democrats in voting for the measure. One Democrat left before his name was called, and one Republican was ill and unable to attend the session.

Opposition to the bill hinged mainly on the charge that the measure was politically inspired. One legislator, Sen. Edward E. Laughlin, a Freeport Republican, claimed that Stevenson was trying to "ram this down people's throats." He told me he didn't think the bill would get more than ten votes "if it weren't for politics." He also questioned exemption of churches under the terms of the bill, demanding to know why they were not included. Laughlin also claimed that certain appropriations bills were being held up by Democrats pending action on FEPC, but he was unable to back up this charge by naming any specific bills.

Another legislator, Republican Sen. Charles Carpentier, who was from East Moline, was more blunt. He tagged the bill "a phony, cheap political proposition!"

Sen. T. MacDowning, a Macomb Republican, was one of the few legislators to explain honestly the quandary facing him on this highly emotional issue.

"I believe in the principles of the bill and can see no harm in it," he said, "but my duty is to represent the people in my district and they seem to disagree with my views."

Speaking for the bill, Sen. Abraham Lincoln Marovitz, a Chicago Democrat who went on later to become a judge in that city, asserted that Stevenson had tried to keep his pledge on FEPC "even though he has alienated men in his own party."

Listening to the debate on the intercom in his statehouse office, Stevenson must have wondered. The vote was so close, the victory almost his—and he sorely needed one. In the press box, we didn't wonder. Neither of the two renegade Democrats—the one who left before his name was called and the one who joined the Republicans—had been contacted by any of Stevenson's aides in advance to determine if anything could be done to change their minds. Nor had several of the Republicans, who might have been swayed into voting for the bill. And, perhaps most importantly, we knew of no action on the part of Stevenson's aides to contact and persuade key civic leaders in the communities represented by legislators openly hostile to the bill. It seemed obvious to us that Stevenson sadly lacked legislative help when it came to the facts of political life.

A bill appropriating $34 million for cities on a per capita grant basis died on the Senate calendar after sales tax extension legislation was trounced by the senators. Another of Stevenson's inaugural address proposals—merger of the Illinois Public Aid Commission with the Public Welfare Department—was killed 18 to 25 in the Senate.

Stevenson endorsed bills sponsored by the Chicago Crime Commission to lengthen grand jury terms, make convictions for perjury easier to obtain and crack down on surprise alibis in criminal court cases. They were beaten.

He also endorsed a bill to raise the gasoline tax from three to five cents a gallon to provide revenue for highway construction work recommended by a highways and traffic problems commission. The bill was decisively defeated in the House after squeaking through the Senate by one vote.

He did get the legislature to adopt a "gateway amendment" resolution providing for submission of as many as three constitutional changes at an election. And his mining laws revision bills were passed. Also, the Republicans were happy to lend their votes to a bill to take the State Police out of politics by putting them under a merit system. Stevenson had recommended this over the protests of the Democrats who had counted on throwing out all the Republican-sponsored cops and putting in their own men. The legislators also raised salaries of state officials, authorized horse racing at night and, of course, passed the "cat bill."

As the final insult, they connived to keep the legislature indefinitely in session instead of adjourning "sine die" so that they could embarrass Stevenson by overriding his vetoes. In that final stormy session, well into the morning of the next day, we were all taken by surprise when Stevenson dredged up an old law involving "prorogue" which he used to adjourn the legislature on grounds that the two houses could not agree on the matter. At least, he closed on a spectacular note.

Despite all the frantic activity of those final days, he also managed to find time to sign a deposition dated June 2 attesting to the good character of Alger Hiss when he had known him years earlier. When the *Chicago Tribune* broke the story, Stevenson was actually at a loss to understand why they or anybody else expected him to have done otherwise. This was his assessment of Hiss at the time, based on a casual acquaintance, as he pointed out.

"What would they have me do—tell a lie?" he retorted coldly when called for a quote. "My deposition stands."

Actually, I could never find anything incriminating in the deposition, which was taken by a United States Commissioner named William B. Chittenden pursuant to an order of the U.S. District Court for the Southern District of New York.

After swearing to tell the truth, identifying himself and listing his various jobs since 1933, Stevenson testified that he had known Hiss since June or July of that year. He said they had served together in the Legal Division of the Agricultural Adjustment Administration in Washington.

"Our contact was frequent but not close nor daily," he said in a rambling statement. "I had no further contact with him until I met him again in the State Department at the end of February or early March to the end of April when Mr. Hiss left for the San Francisco conference. He was, I think, largely preoccupied with the arrangements for that conference, for the United Nations conference on international organization at San Francisco."

Stevenson went on to say that during that interval, he was engaged in other matters and met Hiss mostly in intradepartmental meetings and in connection with aspects of the plan for the conference, largely relating to press relations.

"I was at the conference myself," he said, "as assistant to the secretary of state from about the 10th of May until the end of June. During that interval, Mr. Hiss was secretary general of the conference and I was attached to the United States delegation. Our paths did not cross in a business way, but we met occasionally at official social functions.

"Back in Washington during July, I had some conferences with him in connection with preparations for the presentation of the United Nations charter to the Senate for ratification.

"I resigned from the department early in August, 1945, and so far as I recall I did not meet Mr. Hiss personally again until he came to London in January, 1946, with the United States Delegation to the First General Assembly of the United Nations. During that conference in January and February, we had offices nearby each other and met frequently at delegation meetings and staff conferences.

"I returned to the United States in March, 1946 and I do not believe I met Mr. Hiss again until the United Nations General Assembly in New York in 1947. At that time he was connected with the Carnegie Endowment for International Peace and I visited with him on one or two occasions at my office in the United States Delegation Headquarters in connection with the budget for the United Nations, which was one of my responsibilities as a member of the American Delegation. I have not seen him since."

At this point occurred the dialogue with which his political detractors took issue:

QUESTION: Have you known other persons who have known Mr. Alger Hiss?

ANSWER: Yes.

QUESTION: From the speech of those persons, can you state what the reputation of Alger Hiss is for integrity, loyalty and veracity?

ANSWER: Yes.

QUESTION: Specify whether his reputation for integrity is good or bad.

ANSWER: Good.

QUESTION: Specify whether his reputation for loyalty is good or bad.

ANSWER: Good.

QUESTION: Specify whether his reputation for veracity is good or bad.

ANSWER: Good.

Following these questions and answers, cross interrogatories in behalf of the United States of America, Complainant in said cause, took place:

QUESTION: Were you ever a guest in the home of defendant Alger Hiss at any time in 1935, to and including 1938?

ANSWER: No, I have never been a guest in Mr. Hiss's home.

QUESTION: Did you, prior to 1948, hear that the defendant Alger Hiss during the years 1937 and 1938 removed confidential and secret documents from the State Department and made such documents available to persons not authorized to see or receive them?

ANSWER: No.

QUESTION: Did you, prior to 1948, hear reports that the defendant Alger Hiss was a Communist sympathizer?

ANSWER: No.

QUESTION: State whether or not you ever attended Harvard College or Harvard Law School?

ANSWER: Harvard Law School, September, 1922, to June, 1924.

QUESTION: State whether or not you ever attended Princeton University.

ANSWER: Yes, September, 1918, to June, 1922.

Some time after the deposition, Stevenson told the press in response to questions that he had been asked by Hiss's lawyers to testify as to Hiss's reputation and had agreed to do so but had declined to go to New York. He pointed out that Hiss's reputation with the government obviously had been a good one or he would not have been in such a high post.

Stevenson obviously was irked by the furor over the deposition and repeated that he had told the truth and that he felt it was a basic responsibility of every citizen to testify under such circumstances. He also demanded to know what his critics had expected him to do.

"If I were asked to answer the same questions tomorrow," he said, "in all honesty I would have to give exactly the same answers; and also I would have just as little cause to quarrel with the final verdict of the court."

Still, the *Tribune* wrapped this around his neck. Richard Nixon was to use it as a campaign issue three years later, and I was to wonder why and how the Hamlet bit got started. From my conversations with Stevenson, I felt that he showed no hesitancy in acting—and acting decisively—once he had studied the available facts.

One evening during a heated discussion with the newsmen in the Leland Tavern about a bill pending in the Senate, I became so excited that I left the table, dialed the mansion number and asked Stevenson if he realized the full wrath with which the *Chicago Tribune* would pursue him should he veto the bill.

"Oh, I don't think the *Tribune* can do anything really bad to me," he replied breezily. "I would rather you not quote me just now, however. This is off the record, I take it?"

I assured him that it was, but that I was worried because he was so new on the scene and might not realize all the ramifications involved. He pointed out that I wasn't exactly an old timer in news work.

"But that's very nice of you to worry about me," he said. "Besides, I do have problems."

Then he proceeded to tell me about a little old lady who had been snowing him under with letters complaining that a green cloud was following her around. She wanted him to do something about it.

"She called me just a few minutes ago," he said, "and I came up with an inspired thought. I told her not to worry because the cloud would disappear as soon as it rains. Because, you know, Pat, it has to rain some time!"

It wasn't until I hung up that I wondered if he had been comparing me to the lady with the green cloud.

Early in my Springfield days, I learned that it was traditional for John Dreiske to get into a fight with a legislator at least once every session. Tagge referred to it as Dreiske's "Biennial Battle" and we once spent considerable time in the pressroom drawing up elaborate plans to commemorate this event appropriately with some kind of ceremony. Somebody suggested a statue of Dreiske on the statehouse lawn, which could be the site of speeches and wreath laying and similar activity in keeping with the solemnity of the occasion. But John came up with an even better idea. He suggested that after his demise, he be stuffed and placed on a pedestal in the pressroom. He even jumped up onto a ledge there and stood stiffly and silently staring down at us to demonstrate the full effect. We had to admit it was impressive.

"Once a year," he decreed, "you peasants can gather reverently at my pedestal and pay tribute to me with appropriate speeches of praise."

Instead of laying a wreath, he went on, we would raise our glasses to him in a special toast. Some months earlier, it seems, a small-time Chicago hoodlum named Krazierny* had been taken on a one-way ride to that old City Hall in the sky and never a trace of his remains had been found. That is, until Tagge accidentally dropped a cocktail onion into a bottle of booze in the pressroom. The onion began to disintegrate in the liquid and shortly assumed the rather repulsive effect of a decaying eyeball. Tagge, who was intrigued, began to refer to the bottle as "Old Krazierny." It made me a little ill, but nobody else seemed to mind when he asked politely, "Would you care for a little Krazierny?"

In outlining his elaborate memorial plans, Dreiske decided that our annual toast to him would be with "Old Krazierny" and that the bottle should be stashed away for the occasion. His motion was passed unanimously when he declared us all out of order and proclaimed the meeting over.

In this 1949 session his "Biennial Battle" involved a vivisection bill in which more stray dogs and cats would be made available for medical research. The measure would have re-

---

* Not real name.

quired local dog pound authorities to turn over unclaimed animals to medical research and similar institutions licensed by the health department to obtain them. A detention period of at least ten days—or longer, if city officials desired it— would be required before an animal was considered unclaimed.

Antivivisection proponents descended upon the legislature en masse from all over the country. In addition, two of the Chicago newspapers took opposing editorial views and began to beat the drums with gusto. The *Chicago Herald-American* (being Hearst owned) was angrily against the bill, claiming that it would result in "wholesale slaughter" of pets, not to mention subjecting them to various experimental tortures. On the other side, the *Chicago Sun-Times* held forth in favor of the bill on grounds that human lives would be saved as the result of medical experiments on animals.

A torrent of mail poured in on the legislators—one representative, Mrs. Bernice T. Van Der Vries, a Winnetka Republican, showed me a letter calling her a dirty rat and admonishing her to "watch your step while you are alone."

When the bill came up for debate on the floor of the House, the oratory exploded with particular emphasis on the part of the newspapers involved. One of the legislators, Rep. Clinton J. Searle, a Rock Island Republican and opponent of the bill, stood up to announce:

"There is a private saloon in the pressroom on the third floor of the statehouse, directly over the governor's office! It has a sign out in front which says 'Press Only, Private, No Admittance.' But the older members of the legislature are able to go in and find the icebox all equipped!"

We were in our press boxes watching and listening— including Dreiske—when Searle went on to refer to John as the "private bartender for that saloon."

There was nothing he could do at the time because Searle was speaking from the floor of the House, but back in the pressroom he went to work immediately on an official statement, which he wrote and rewrote and edited and finally read aloud to us:

"Searle's reference to me apparently is made because I happen to be the president of the Illinois Legislative Correspondents Association. His reference also is to a workroom, in every sense of the word. In this workroom, twenty-five newspapermen and women are in and out up to eighteen hours a day in covering the Illinois legislature."

Tagge wanted to add to the statement that "Besides, all we drink here is 'Old Krazierny' which is pure as the driven snow" but Dreiske wouldn't let him.

Searle never responded to Dreiske's statement and the vivisection bill was subsequently defeated.

After the adjournment of the legislature, Stevenson had little time to bind up his wounds. He spent most of his summer poring over bills which had been passed, signing some, vetoing some, permitting some to become law without his signature. Occasionally he played a little tennis at a local country club and a few desultory rounds of golf. Ellen Stevenson had returned to their Libertyville home and there was talk of a separation. As far as we could tell, the two had been separated unofficially for some time, but nobody would confirm this.

If there was a dearth of news from the mansion, however, the Illinois State Fair provided enough to divert us from Stevenson's personal life. While making a routine check on news sources one day, I ran into U.S. District Attorney Howard Doyle, who was dying to tell somebody—just anybody!—that fan dancer Sally Rand was in town.

"You know that guy that Stevenson appointed agricultural director?" he asked me.

I knew. Roy Yung—a bespectacled, very cautious type of gentleman who was even more suspicious of the press than Stevenson.

"Well!" said Howard importantly. "It seems he has just told Sally that she can't appear at the state fair after all, as she had planned. It seems that the party of the first part, Mr. Roy Yung, does not appreciate the esthetic appeal or artistic aspects of the dancing performed by the party of the second part, to-wit, Miss Sally Rand. I think he is afraid that all the young men who come from all over Illinois to the fair to look at cows and pigs will be lured into seeing her, instead, and will then return to their communities to live lives of shame and degradation."

"How'd you find out about this?" I asked.

"Easy. She has just consulted with an attorney about filing a lawsuit against Mr. Roy Yung, and the lawyer happens to be a friend of mine."

Surprisingly enough, I discovered that Sally Rand had checked in at the Lincoln Hotel under her real name. Usually, we received tips from hotel workers about the arrivals of celebrities, but the desk clerk had not recognized the name. When I reached Sally with a phone call and told her what I had discovered, she was aghast.

"Oh, don't print that!" she gasped. "Please don't print that! If you do, you might ruin everything!"

I didn't want to ruin anything for her or anybody else, I told her, but if she had been banned from performing at the state fair, this was news.

"But I haven't," she said. "I mean, not really. I think Mr. Yung is going to change his mind and if you print anything about it, he'll be perfectly furious because he wants to keep this quiet."

By the time she had finished describing the rigors of fan dancing on the state fair circuit and the amount of money she would lose if she lost her booking in Illinois, I was beginning to feel pretty sympathetic towards her. And when she explained that she was struggling to support a young son, I gave in and agreed to hold off on the story, provided she call me before leaving Springfield and let me know what happened.

"I want the story exclusively," I insisted, "which is only fair."

She promised she would.

She didn't. She just left town a day later.

When I called Yung, he almost passed out from shock, but he admitted that he had officially ruled Sally was a "no no" at the fair, and I hastily sent out a story on the wire beginning:

Springfield, Ill., July 10—(INS)—Sally Rand, with or without fans, was banned today from appearing at the Illinois State Fair.

When the story appeared in print, I expected an unhappy reaction from Yung and I got it. What I didn't expect was an angry phone call from Detroit from Sally, who was perfectly furious and who threatened to come back to Springfield, invade my office and make me very sorry I had written that story—even though it happened to be true. She was so mad at me, in fact, that I thought I ought to call the INS bureau in Chicago, explain what had happened and ask for advice. The editor who took the call wasn't much help.

"If she comes into your office," he said, "let us know what she says and does. It'll make a good follow-up story."

When a newsman on the *Illinois State Register* saw my story on the wire, he was so fascinated that he printed the following poem accompanying the story:

> We hear this cry on every hand —
> In every street and alley:
> "Why do they bar our Sally Rand?
> Oh, give us fan-clad Sally!
>
> We need her, in this torrid heat,
> To bring her breezy blessing —
> To show us what, from head to feet,
> Is proper summer dressing!
>
> Oh, what a cooling style is this
> That Sally's noted for —
> A garment which insures real bliss —
> A fan — and — nothing more!"
>
> Roy E. Yung, the State Fair Chief,
> Replies to those who rally
> With fanfare for this fan relief;
> "No, boys! You can't have Sally!"

> Yung to fan-dancing puts a check,
> And Sally's dance charms bans!
> But, Roy! When it's hot as heck
> Why can't we have her fans?

I didn't save my story, but I saved the poem. Despite my inexperience in journalism, I knew that there wasn't much of *that* kind of writing going around.

When I related this incident to Stevenson later, he was greatly interested to learn that his new agriculture director was so concerned about the morals of Illinois' fairgoers. He also seemed a bit regretful when he mused:

"She was once quite a drawing card, you know. Before your time, of course, but every young man wanted to see her dance. I don't suppose she would create as much of a sensation as Roy thinks."

"What about you?" I asked him. "Would you like to have seen her?"

He eyed me suspiciously.

"At least you don't think I'm too old," he finally said, "or you wouldn't have asked."

Once or twice in conversation, he had made a point that he was approaching fifty, and had quoted the comment that "It's not so bad when you consider the alternative."

His age was weighing on him, but I assumed that it was just a normal reaction.

As things turned out, we got another drawing card at the Illinois State Fair who was almost as good as Sally Rand, depending upon whether one preferred fan dancers or romantic vice presidents. Old Alben Barkley, who was a very distant cousin of Stevenson's, had just launched his courtship of Jane Hadley in St. Louis and on August 18 he came to Springfield to speak at the fair. Stevenson introduced him to the crowd and I sent out the following story:

Springfield, Ill., Aug. 18—(INS)—Five thousand Democrats attending Governor's Day at the State Fair today got a glimpse of Vice President Alben Barkley's heart on his sleeve.

Adlai Stevenson and then Vice-President Alben Barkley greet the crowd at the Illinois State Fair. Photo courtesy Chicago Sun-Times.

Gov. Adlai E. Stevenson introduced the vice president and extended an invitation to him to come back to next year's fair. He noted that "Springfield isn't so very far from St. Louis," (home of Mrs. Carleton Hadley, 38-year-old widow toward whom Barkley is reported romantically inclined).

The 71-year-old Barkley promptly accepted, and wistfully added a wish that in the meantime "somebody will do something about moving Springfield closer to St. Louis, or St. Louis closer to Springfield."

He commented: "Those of you who have not yet experienced it cannot realize the pain I suffer by being so near and yet so far."

Afterwards at the mansion, I asked Barkley if he intended to marry Mrs. Hadley.

"Don't you think that's rather an impertinent question?" he asked.

"No, I don't," I told him honestly.

"Well, I realize you're under some compunction from your editor to ask me," he conceded, and then went into his most charming act thanking me for dropping by to see him (as if it were a social call) and expressing his regrets that he had no comment at present about anything except the beautiful weather we were having and what a lovely girl I was!!

While we fenced verbally, Stevenson stood by with a rather disinterested look on his face.

A few weeks later, he introduced Barkley again to a Springfield audience—this time at a life insurance company ceremony at which the Veep was the main speaker, and it was obvious that he was deeply preoccupied. His introduction was prosaic and his "witticisms" downright lame.

On September 30, Stevenson issued the following statement:

"I am deeply distressed that due to the incompatibility of our lives, Mrs. Stevenson feels a separation is necessary. Although I don't believe in divorce, I will not contest it. We have separated with the highest mutual regard."

There was considerable speculation as to what *really* happened. Nobody believed that after so many years of marriage, the Stevensons would suddenly find themselves incompatible. I didn't share that opinion. Stevenson's married life seemed to have consisted of tripping around the country pursuing a career in government while Ellen kept the old home fires burning, and I didn't see how they stayed married as long as they had.

From what I heard about her, she was an extraordinarily intelligent woman and a gifted writer of poetry. My brief meeting with her at the mansion on the night of the press party left me with the impression of a wife who was as strong-willed as her husband. It struck me that Adlai and Ellen might have been too much alike to get along well . . . perhaps not alike in tastes, necessarily, but in temperament and ambition.

At the time, people seemed to feel that Ellen looked down her nose on his political friends and wanted him back up in Libertyville acting the role of country gentleman. Maybe so. But whatever, there was never any scandal involved—no other party in the case—and the whole affair was just another tragic event in the life of a man who was brilliant but probably maddeningly difficult to get along with.

When the official announcement was made that the Veep and Jane Hadley were going to get married, International News Service promptly assigned me to cover the event in St. Louis. After all, weddings were "women's news," I was a woman, and therefore automatically qualified to do the job. What INS didn't know was that I was almost totally ignorant of fashions, I had very little clothes sense, I had difficulty recognizing any but the most vivid hues, and I had never covered a wedding in my life.

The Associated Press girl, Milcie Sloboda Lane, was almost as horrified as I was when the assignment came through.

"Gads!" she exclaimed in disbelief. And then, with her customary practical, down-to-earth, sensible approach, she added briskly:

"Well, we've got one week to teach you something."

During that week, she hauled me around all over Springfield's downtown section from store window to store window, pointing, describing, moving on, then returning and asking me to describe what I saw.

"No, no," she would say patiently, "it's not a tuck—it's a pinch pleat. And it's tangerine, not orange."

At the end of my crash course in fashion design, she loaned me her shortie fur coat, put me on a train to St. Louis, waved good-bye shouting "Don't worry!" and then, as she told me later, went home and prayed for me.

The ceremony was scheduled for November 18 before a small group of close friends and relatives in the oak-paneled Singleton Memorial Chapel of St. John's Methodist Church at 5000 Washington Boulevard. But the activities started the preceding afternoon when I joined a crowd of reporters, photographers, sightseers and airport personnel at Lambert Airport for Barkley's arrival from Washington. It was a cold, blustery day and the plane, due in at 2:14, was reported late.

Jane Hadley arrived in a $3,300 black Oldsmobile convertible which was Barkley's wedding gift to her, and when she saw the crowd, exclaimed "My word!" and ran into the Eastern Airlines freight office to hide.

"No comment!" she kept saying to us as we chased her all the way. "I've devoted four days to the press and this is MY day!"

The bride-to-be didn't appear happy with any of us and when Barkley finally arrived, she told him acidly that "we're well chaperoned" and suggested they hurry to the car and take off. In the meantime, the Secret Service agents accompanying Barkley trotted along beside them, holding everyone at bay except me. For some reason, they thought I was with the Barkley entourage and I was able to walk along right behind the couple, listening in on their conversation while the photographers snapped pictures of us all.

Fortunately for me, a publicity agent who had been assigned to handle the wedding details for the press, showered us with handouts from beginning to end, including one way-out news release about Mrs. Hadley's "going away" outfit which began: "Anthony Blotta looked to the East, translated the princely garb of India into this handsome gray wool coat dress, touched with midnight blue velvet at collar and sahib cuffs."

This was of no help at all to the *Chicago Sun-Times* report-.er. In a burst of genius, the paper had assigned a former war correspondent to the wedding with instructions to write his own original copy and not depend on the handouts. He obeyed. In describing the bride's "going away" outfit, he said that it was a "sort of battleship gray."

And when it came to her wedding suit, all the lessons which Milcie had given me were for naught. According to the publicity man, the suit, designed by Hattie Carnegie, was of "Barkley Blue," a specially created color (how Hattie invented a new color, I don't know), and the tucks were not pinch pleats but "nips in" at the waistline.

However, my lack of experience would not have hampered me much, anyhow, inasmuch as the entire affair turned into more of a fiasco than a formal ceremony, thanks to the avidity with which the press scrabbled for every scrap of information to the point of silliness. After the wedding rehearsal the evening before, when Barkley emerged from the chapel, he gamely told us that he was "cool as a cucumber." Within minutes, we relayed this world-shaking quote to our offices and then rushed back to count the pews in the chapel (28), the candles on the altar (also 28), the windows (8) and the altar steps (3).

One of the reporters got hold of a member of the rehearsal party and scooped us all with the fascinating disclosure that Barkley had turned to the left instead of the right at one point, but that he finally got it down correctly. I managed to redeem myself by grabbing a woman who had made a special trip to the chapel to present the wedding certificate to the bridal party.

"I understand you made a special trip here to present the wedding certificate to the couple," I said to her.

"Yes," she beamed happily. "My name is Mrs. Ruby Koelling—K-O-E-L-L-I-N-G and I'm Recorder of Deeds at City Hall. I made a special trip here to present the wedding certificate to the couple."

"How did everything go?" I asked her.

"Just fine."

"Who did you give the certificate to?"

"I don't know. Somebody took it."

I called in the story that Mrs. Ruby Koelling, Recorder of Deeds at City Hall, had made a special trip to the chapel to present the wedding certificate to the bridal party and that she was thrilled to be a part of such an historic and happy event. I also mentioned that there was a canopy outside the chapel.

"What color is it?" asked the newsman who was taking my story.

"Green."

When my story was printed, an item was added that the interview with Mrs. Koelling had taken place under a specially constructed green canopy outside the chapel.

On the morning of the wedding day (cloudy with temperatures in the upper thirties prevailing with a forecast of a rise to about fifty in the afternoon, according to the reporter who called the weather bureau), we crowded into the chapel along with thirty-three members of the immediate family of the couple and several close friends. There were at least fifty of us—writers, photographers, telecasters and radio men—permitted inside the chapel, and a bevy of TV cameramen representing the then four major networks which had scheduled nationwide broadcasts outside the chapel. A twenty-four station hookup had been set up in the home of Mr. and Mrs. T. M. Sayman at 5399 Lindell Boulevard, where the reception after the wedding was scheduled. The ceremony was over in seven minutes and, I thought, went off nicely as weddings go. The first vice president of the United States to be married while in office performed his role without a hitch and everything went smoothly until they emerged from the chapel into a crowd estimated later at five thousand.

Movie cameras whirred, spectators jostled one another, the Secret Service men went wild trying to protect the couple from their well-wishers, sightseers began shoving forward screaming and howling and, as the couple barely managed to hustle inside their car and make a getaway, the crowd thundered into the chapel, almost trampling us.

As I ducked behind a pew, several people galloped past, nearly toppling a large urn to the floor. Bent on souvenirs, they grabbed everything that was movable, stripping the altar of the chrysanthemums and ferns which had served as decorations. Some of the gleeful scavengers rushed out of the chapel waving their trophies and shouting to the others to go in and help themselves. The poor decorator, Edward Burkhardt, stood there watching his painstaking work demolished in minutes, shaking his head in dismay and repeating in a tone of astonishment: "This is most unusual, most unusual, most unusual!"

I was beginning to understand the bride's attitude toward publicity. When they had emerged from the chapel, she was overheard to say: "I hate to go out in all that mess!" whereupon, as we reporters gleefully noted, the Veep had replied: "That's not a mess, dear—that's the American public."

In view of what had happened, I was on her side—they were a mess. However, my opinion of the bride's friends, the Saymans, wasn't particularly flattering when I arrived for the reception and found myself, along with the other reporters, relegated to the basement of the house for a repast of beer and hot dogs while the celebrants dined on lobster, ham, champagne and similar gourmet fare in the dining room on the main floor. We had not expected to eat with the wedding party. But neither had we expected to be doled out beer and hot dogs! Stomping back upstairs, we announced that we would just wait in the living room.

Poor Barkley was distressed. With his innate kindness, he insisted that each of us at least receive a piece of the huge, two-tier wedding cake when it was cut—and he came out into the living room to distribute the pieces personally to us.

Conditions were near bedlam throughout the house with radio announcers wandering around thrusting microphones before unsuspecting guests, photographers setting off flash bulbs almost every second, and television lights glaring in the background. We followed the couple right out to their car, waving good-bye and shouting questions to which the

Veep kept shouting back: "We're going to Shangri-La!"* And, all of a sudden, they were gone and the big national story of the day was over and we were busy calling taxis and heading back to our offices to write the windup.

I was going to save my piece of wedding cake to give to Milcie, but on the way back to Springfield on the train, I got hungry and ate it. Instead, I gave her a clipping of the photograph from the front page of the *St. Louis Globe Democrat* showing the Veep, the bride and me at the airport.

"Just think!" she said when she saw it. "My shortie coat— on the front page!"

A few days later, a newspaper friend sent me a front page from the *New York Journal-American* with my by-line story bannered and a note scrawled across it: "Pat, you hit the big time!"

For several weeks, I kept waiting for INS to promote me to the New York office or make me their new star roving reporter or something like that, but nothing happened and I was back at grinding out prep basketball scores and plodding along in the traces again, and I decided that they were probably saving me for the next time a vice president of the United States decided to get married while in office. That was the way INS operated.

* Which turned out to be Sea Island, Georgia.

A portion of the gambling devices confiscated during the famous "gambling raids" of the Stevenson administration. Photo courtesy Chicago Sun-Times.

CHAPTER FOUR

"Which Way Is the Gambling Raid? . . . And Who Done It?"

Although Stevenson's second year in office was not exactly of vintage quality, it wasn't boring—thanks to his former campaign staffer, big roaring Louis Ruppel.

Aside from the brief campaign weeks spent riding around Illinois in the summer of 1948, Stevenson and Ruppel had seen nothing of each other. So much mystery surrounded Ruppel's short-lived stint on the campaign that I sometimes wondered what had happened. However, the two men were still on speaking terms because after Stevenson's victory, Ruppel wrote the new governor on November 5 from his Chicago address:

> Dear Adlai:
> Nice going, Governor! I am sure the people of Illinois will have no regrets in their choice for the next four years.
> All of the best.
> Sincerely,
> (signed) Louis

Two days later, Stevenson had shot back an answer:

> Dear Lou:
> Thanks for your note. I have not forgotten what you did for me and when given a little time I may be able to make the past less barren.
> Sincerely,
> (signed) Adlai

On December 1, Stevenson wrote Ruppel again:

> Dear Lou:
> We are getting the house in order at last and, thanks to some last minute relief, I am enclosing a check—which is both inadequate and late. But I am sure you know that my sincere thanks go with it.
>
> Sincerely yours,
(signed) Adlai
>
> P.S. Miss Evans* tells me that I am also indebted to you for the three splendid flags which have backed me up in fair weather and foul. Thanks again!

Stevenson, of course, was referring to the money due Ruppel for his work on the campaign—$1,200 a month. Back in May of 1948 at the height of his campaign he had written Ruppel asking the former newspaper editor to get in touch with him. After the two had met and talked things over, Ruppel had quoted his price and on May 8 of that year, Stevenson had written him:

> Mr. Louis Ruppel
> 438 West Briar Place
> Chicago, Illinois
>
> Dear Lou:
> I have done some telephoning today but not too successfully. There was some demurrer about the $1200 per month, and I wish we could start at the same rate that Jim Mulroy was on—$1,000. But if that is the best you feel you can do I think it is safe to assume that the group, when I can contact them, will all agree on the understanding that you will be paid at that rate if, as and when the money becomes available by contributions and without any first priority.

* Stevenson's secretary, Miss Carol Evans.

60

Such an arrangement is unsatisfactory but I see no other way of doing it, and I am reasonably confident that with anything like the sort of response which many anticipate, the money should be available. I think we should have the further understanding that if the arrangement does not prove satisfactory to either of us it can be terminated on a month's notice. I can well imagine that if you have worked for a month or so and it becomes more and more apparent that it will be difficult or impossible to pay you at this rate that you may want to discontinue.

You need have no apprehension on the score of Jim Mulroy. I have talked with him and he would welcome the association, leaving him to direct the activities of the non-partisan committee.

As I told you, I am leaving now and will be back here on the 17th for three or four days. Perhaps you should plan to get in touch with me then and start to work if this sort of a loose arrangement is satisfactory to you. Meanwhile if you want to come in and talk to Morrill, Epple and Miss Evans, please do so. I have told them that you might want to look things over and get a little familiar with what has transpired and what is contemplated.

Hastily yours,

(signed) Adlai E. Stevenson

Ruppel responded with a letter which read, in part:

While I have never made a deal like this, which you so genially describe as a "sort of loose arrangement," I am happy to join up. Furthermore, my only worry now is that we get nice weather for the inauguration. See you Monday.

He didn't have to worry long. When inauguration time came, he wasn't invited.

Four months after Stevenson took the oath of office, Ruppel had popped up again in the news—this time as editor of *Collier's* magazine and obviously in another of those Little Nell cliff-hanger situations involving a slowly dying publication.

("They always give me something nobody else wants," he had told me once.)

Collier's circulation was up then (3,300,000), but the quality of the magazine was poor and the publisher, Ed Anthony, wanted a "personality" to liven things up. He certainly found it in Ruppel.

Throughout Stevenson's first year as governor, there was obviously no hard feeling between him and Ruppel because in August, the *Collier's* editor wrote him:

> Dear Adlai:
> I went over to New Jersey the other day in the 97° temperature on a little matter of editorial business with Admiral Bowen at the Thomas Alva Edison Foundation.
> I was delightfully surprised to see your picture on the wall.
> The Admiral is a grand guy and I had a pleasant visit—I have made a wonderful new friend.
> I told him that you were taking much better pictures nowadays and that I was going to write you and ask you to send him one of your newer ones.
> All of the best to you, the family and Jim Mulroy.
>   Sincerely,
>   (signed) Louis Ruppel

And back came Stevenson's genial reply:

> Dear Lou:
> Many thanks for your letter. I am delighted that you met Hal Bowen. He is a great guy and good company.
> My best to you and my congratulations on the Ruppelized Colliers!
>   Sincerely yours,
>   (signed) Adlai

A few months later, Ruppel took careful aim and shot down the bluebirds of happiness that had been winging between the two men carrying these affable little notes. On April 15, 1950 the new "Ruppelized" *Collier's* came out with the first of two blistering exposes on gambling in Illinois titled: "ILLINOIS SHAKEDOWN: The Little Guys Lose."

To make sure that nobody missed the point, Ruppel had printed three photos of Illinois Atty. Gen. Ivan Elliott, Adams County State's Atty. John T. Reardon and Gov. Adlai Stevenson. Over Adlai's photo were the words (in red ink) "I CAN'T!" and the squib:

"Governor Adlai Stevenson won the support of Republicans and Democrats on reforms, but he has not yet delivered on gambling."

Although most of the article zeroed in on gambling in the city of Quincy, there were several juicy little paragraphs by the author, Gordon Schendel, to the effect that Stevenson was reneging on his campaign promises. Schendel quoted from some of Adlai's speeches, particularly one delivered on Democratic Day at the 1948 Illinois State Fair, in which Stevenson asserted:

"My colleagues and I are going to fumigate the statehouse or break our hearts in the attempt!"

Stevenson also was quoted as admitting that gambling was his Number One headache but that it was a "local problem" to be solved by local law officials.

Even more telling were quotes from Stevenson's sidekick, Attorney General Elliott, to the effect that his powers were limited by statute and that he could move into a county only when asked to by local authorities.

Schendel went on to say that newspapermen in Springfield were making wry jokes about how much worse the slot machine situation would have to become before the governor would use his legal powers to act.

I didn't know about that but from personal observation, I knew that the slots and punchboards were in operation full blast all over middle Illinois, as they had been since the day I moved there. I was not much of a gambler myself, but some of the newsmen with whom I lunched played the punchboards regularly, and one of them rolled the dice for "double or nothing" almost every noon (and lost). We usually ate in a narrow little place called "The Saddle Club," where the beer was cold and the plate lunches adequate. At the time, their chief cook was a chubby little woman named Mary Jane who got high as she cooked and turned out odd combinations like coddled oysters on toast and carameled potato cake. During holiday seasons, she would pour half a bottle of rum into a mince pie, drink the rest and come wobbling out, bearing her masterpiece and singing "Joy to the World." Sometimes she did this when there wasn't any holiday season going on.

The rest of the time she took orders for drinks, greatly endearing herself to us one day when we heard this exchange between her and the bartender:

"One creme de menthe!" she yelled.

"Frappe?" he asked.

"I don't know his name! He just asked for a creme de menthe!"

Between Mary Jane and the slot machines (not to mention the little guy with the green eyeshade operating the dice table at the rear of the tavern) we enjoyed the place.

In fact, I do not recall many places in Springfield which did not offer some type of gambling—and nobody thought a thing about it, despite the fact that gambling had been illegal in Illinois since 1895. None of the newspapers published anything about it and nobody appeared to question it.

When Ruppel's article slamming Stevenson appeared in *Collier's,* the effect in the executive mansion was instant horror. They couldn't very well deny it. On the other hand, they didn't particularly care to confirm it, and for several days nobody was available for comment one way or the other.

The best they could come up with was a "don't quote me but it's just a personal feud." Ruppel was mad at Stevenson, they said, because he hadn't been paid what he thought was coming to him from the campaign. Curious, I wrote Ruppel asking him what he was doing to our "dark horse" governor.* Back came the prompt reply:

* Contrary to popular notion, as far back as 1950, Adlai Stevenson was being talked about as a dark horse possibility for the presidency.

Which Way is the Gambling Raid?

Dear Pat:

I'm an editor, Darling. The statements put out in answer to the piece sure lack fire. The issue out this Friday will really make them jump. Off the record to you the personal feud statement is silly. That I didn't get paid all they owed me wasn't Stevenson's fault because, as I understand it, they didn't have the money. I like the guy, but then I liked the late Jimmy Walker, too. But governors and mayors and other elected officials who make promises to do things just ought to do them, that's all.

And, frankly, Darling, I don't think our boy Adlai is a dark horse or even a palomino. If there are any dark horses from Illinois, you'll have to look toward the Senate where one Paul Douglas enjoys the respect, affection and admiration of all his colleagues, earned by performance.

Finally, Dear, do YOU really think anybody in Springfield would have told us the information we found out by ourselves?

Sincerely,

(signed) Louis

In conjunction with the Friday issue to which Ruppel had referred in his letter to me, Walter Winchell came out with a rat-a-tat-tat to inform Mr. and Mrs. America and all the ships at sea that Ruppel had just completed his first year as editor of *Collier's*.

"When he got the job," said Winchell, "the knockers said he wouldn't last a dozen months. The mag has never been so zingy."

I had a feeling that Stevenson, who was the one who had been zinged, didn't agree, but by that time Ruppel had him hurting and he couldn't ignore it any more than a boxer could shake off a roundhouse right and call off the fight on grounds that he wasn't interested.

It may have been that the ebullient Ruppel expected the matter to end with the publication of the second and final article on Illinois gambling, but instead, one of Stevenson's close friends, historian-columnist Arthur Schlesinger, stepped into the fray with the open charge that Ruppel's part in Stevenson's gubernatorial campaign had been "disastrous."

Almost simultaneously the *Sun-Times'* John Dreiske called it all a "grudge" matter. This time it was Ruppel who started hurting, and he reacted by sending me a sheaf of photostats of personal correspondence between him and Stevenson. His lengthy letter read, in part:

. . . I have concluded that despite Schlesinger's and Dreiske's unfair pokes at me I'm not going to answer them at this time. We expect to win several important awards for 1949 and I'll use those as the answer as to whether or not I run this magazine by "grudge." In sending you these photostats I wish you would take good care not to have them fall into the hands of the wrong people. I give them to you in confidence and not for publication as we agreed.*

I'm afraid the Governor is making a mistake in allowing anyone to put out the "grudge" rumor. If you feel it is necessary in your own interests to show him these photostats, go ahead. For my own part, the record of accomplishments on Collier's is so clear, especially to executives here, that I don't have to apologize. It's quite obvious that I have reported on gambling and criminals and lobbyists in many states, and Illinois is just one of them. One of the best ways of getting fired that I know is to misuse editorial power and in 25 years I have yet to be fired. . . .

The Dreiske and Schlesinger cracks were dirty pool, but they spelled my name correctly and they can't match some of the other poisonous things I've had happen to me in my time. Of course Schlesinger's crack about my part in the Stevenson campaign being disastrous is just too funny. Adlai got elected, didn't he? And I got two-fifths of my promised pay. Does a guy with a "grudge" give a prize set of flags to the Governor? I voted for him and I'd do it again if Green was his opponent. And, if Adlai can be a Democrat and own half of the Republican Bloomington Pantagraph, then I can be a Democrat and campaign against hoodlums and gangsters bleeding the poor and the ignorant with gambling devices in any one of the 48 states. Say, don't you think the way to

---

* In later conversation, Ruppel agreed that the photostats could be published after Stevenson left public office. Ruppel died unexpectedly in New York several years later.

prove it isn't a grudge, that I mean business, is to send a couple of reporters back into Illinois to check up?

I didn't know what to tell Ruppel. I had a feeling that he hoped I would contact Stevenson, show him the photostats and ask him bluntly about the "grudge" rumor. On the other hand, it was obvious that Ruppel trusted me not to release the papers for publication, even though he had blithely handed me an exclusive inside story on the whole business.

I was still speculating as to whether or not to enlighten Stevenson about my spectator role in the matter and get his reaction when he suddenly called out the state police on the first of a series of gambling raids. Immediately, I called him at the mansion and asked him to arrange for me to go along on one of the raids. He agreed and turned the matter over to one of his public relations men who promptly set up a trip for me—and the Springfield managers of the Associated Press and United Press bureaus.

It seemed to me that whenever I had a bright idea, somebody always tossed it out for everyone to enjoy, but whenever one of the men came up with something he got an exclusive and I was left out in the cold.

Once, for want of something better to do, I wrote a statement for Stevenson involving a facetious request by an Indiana Press Club in South Bend. Some of the boys in the back room there had written Stevenson asking his permission to borrow a currently notorious romantic old swindler named Sigmund Engel, who was in prison for conning a long line of widows out of their life savings. They said they wanted Sigmund to lend an appropriate air to their Gridiron Dinner which was to be held on Valentine's Day Eve.

When I saw the news item about their request, I recalled a recent hoax involving a so-called Giant Turtle of Churubusco (Indiana) which had been "seen" by several Hoosiers . . . they said. This gave me an idea. I wrote and sent to Stevenson the following letter for him to send back to the Indiana newsmen:

I was intrigued by your request to "borrow" Mr. Sigmund Engel for your annual Gridiron Dinner to be staged Monday, February 13, at the South Bend Press Club.

Mr. Engel will not be able to appear in your production because he is fulfilling a command performance at the Illinois State Penitentiary at the moment. Should it develop that Mr. Engel can participate in one of your shows in some future year, I hope you will be willing to reciprocate by lending to the Illinois State Museum your famous Giant Turtle of Churubusco, about which we have recently read so much.

Naturally, I assumed that if Stevenson used the letter he would let me know so that I could get off a good news feature about it. I assumed too much. The first I heard that he had sent the letter was when I plodded into my office one early morning to find a frantic message on the wire from Chicago to the effect that Associated Press was carrying a colorful story about Adlai Stevenson and a giant turtle. (Sure enough, there in my mailbox was the letter—in the form of a news release distributed to everybody to hell and gone!)

On the morning of the gambling raid, we three bureau managers received calls to gather at the home of Stevenson's public relations man after telling our Chicago offices we would be out of pocket for a while. The most elaborate precautions were taken to assure the utmost secrecy involving our destination.

In addition, we were given an eight-point list of orders which were to be followed by the police:

1. Cover the device politely and courteously until pickup.
2. Allow no one to remove device, or telephone, until pickup (on threat of arrest). Ask all persons leaving premises to give name and address.
3. Tag each machine with name and address of place where located along with name of owner of place.
4. Obtain name of owner, serviceman and collector on each device, if possible.

5. Proceed to another spot and repeat same on any devices found in open view, until no other devices in public view.

6. Truck all devices to local State's Attorney indicating that each officer confiscating a machine wants to issue a complaint for immediate destruction under Chapter 38, Paragraph 342, Illinois Revised Statutes, and that Attorney General will advise with him on procedure if desired. Complaint should issue from County Court or Circuit Court preferably.

7. No warrants are to be issued against persons, only against machines, unless local State's Attorney requests same before he will authorize warrants against the machines. Warrant will be "People of State of Illinois vs. Slot Machines" and one warrant for each place where machines were seized should be issued on complaint by officer who seized same.

8. No comment to press. Courteous raid against property, not people. No arrests unless absolutely necessary.

Crammed into an unmarked state car with the two other managers, a state photographer, the public relations man and with a plainclothes officer at the wheel, we headed up into northern Illinois, a trip of several hours. Pulling up to a halt just outside the small community of Morris in Grundy County (which just happened coincidentally to be in the political territory of Republican U.S. Sen. Everett McKinley Dirksen), we waited while our driver solemnly checked his watch. Everything was synchronized, he told us. No calls on the police radio were to be made for fear the gamblers were monitoring the air waves. Silently, we waited and watched until the secret zero hour arrived and our driver announced grimly "We're off!" and stepped on the accelerator.

We were still admiring the split-second precision with which everything was coordinated as we sped into the drowsy little town of Morris, roared through the downtown area leaving surprised passersby in our wake, tore on out the other side of town and came to a panting halt in the middle of a cornfield.

"Where the hell's the raid?" the photographer asked.

Our driver shook his head, turned the car around and sped back into town as fast as he could go and on out the other side where we came to a stop again.

"I don't know," he said. "I thought it was on the main drag."

It seems that he didn't even know the name of the place being raided. The photographer had an idea.

"Drive us on into town again, only go slow," he said, "and stop at the first tavern you see."

His scheme worked. When he emerged from the tavern, he gave us directions.

"It was easy," he said, "I just asked them where I could place a bet."

By the time we pulled up in front of a roadhouse called "The Seven Gables" a mile north of the town, fourteen state policemen had already broken in and were busy disposing of thirty-two slot machines, a gambling table, a roulette wheel and several horse race wall boards. The manager of the road-house, leaning resignedly against the bar, asked us politely if we would care for a drink. When the phone rang, he lifted the receiver, listened a moment and then replied with great aplomb:

"No sir, I can't accept any bets today. We're being raided by Adlai Stevenson's police."

Although we didn't know until later, other state police had swooped down on gambling spots throughout a three-county area, confiscating in all some two hundred pieces of gambling equipment which they presented to the state's attorneys in the counties.

Back in Springfield, Governor Stevenson issued a statement:

"The Attorney General and I regret the necessity of these raids on commercialized gambling. The local government should protect its own integrity. Besides, the taxpayers should not have to pay for law enforcement twice."

Shortly after my return to my office, I received a note from Ruppel enclosing a carbon copy of a three-page letter he had written to Adlai Stevenson. From his letter, it was easy to tell what Stevenson had written to him, because Ruppel was furious.

May 15, 1950

Honorable Adlai E. Stevenson
Governor, State of Illinois
Springfield, Illinois

Dear Adlai:

I was sorry to get your letter. You have been badly advised. You know—and the activities of your own state police prove it—that I did not print a "remarkably inaccurate" article about gambling in Illinois. You knew gambling existed when you ran for governor, you know gambling has gone on since you have been governor, and you know gambling will go on until you (as promised) clean it up.

I do not print "remarkably inaccurate" articles. I did not want to print the Illinois articles, but I've been seeking out—all over the country—the base of public corruption. The base is gambling. I've printed articles on Binaggio (a clear warning of rottenness in Kansas City); on Florida and I have articles on other areas still to come. My objective—and that of Collier's—is to do what we think necessary to curb the invisible government backed by gambling billions, which is now growing up in the country—and growing up fast.

I guess you really don't know me even though we rode around the State of Illinois quite a little bit. I'm sorry that your people saw fit to feed two columnists an idea that I bear you a grudge. Nothing could be farther from the truth. I worked for you, I voted for you and I'd vote for you again against Green.

But I am running a national magazine and I am running it in the interest of the whole country with the same aims and effort that I worked for you. I cannot isolate Illinois because you, as Governor, are a friend of mine.

Now, as for your letter of May 2nd. If there were any faults with the story they were technical and minor and not as you say "remarkably inaccurate." You should know that I leave no strings untied. I did a story about conditions in Chicago when I was on the Herald-American in 1945, and in large measure those conditions still exist. I documented that story with photos, affidavits and photostats. I have done the same thing on the story of gambling in Illinois. Now, if the hoodlums close up for a while of their own accord because of this "heat" generated by the Collier's articles, let me assure you you can't depend on them to stay closed. I enclose three photos made in the covering of the story that we did not put in the magazine. These photos are copyrighted and owned by Collier's. Our photographers will be back in those same places again so I'm not mentioning the names of the locations until such time as we can see whether or not the condition has been cleaned up.

As I said, these articles are well documented. I even have a copy of a letter of yours to a state's attorney that would make interesting, if not amusing, reading. I have several affidavits and a copy of one of Ivan Elliott's letters that matches yours in saying that he's against gambling, but the local folks will have to clear it up. Our attitude in being against gambling is what we all are, but the people we elect have got to be not only in accord with us, but the ones to do something about it.

State's Attorney Young of Fulton County may write you his denial of such statements, but that's his word against Gordon Schendel's, and it happens that the same photographer that did your campaign pictures was along on this assignment and can back Schendel's reporting. I also have a letter in my possession addressed to Schendel by State's Attorney Young. It was dated April 8th, but it expressed an entirely different viewpoint. As an indication of our thoroughness we even got releases from Young to use his picture in newspaper ads. You, as a lawyer, I'm sure, will admit that's pulling in all ends. If you think the thing through, you'll see where it would be better for you to turn your state police loose against every gambling device in the state rather than try to discredit Collier's articles.

I know you're busy because obviously you gave little or no attention to our story on Artie Samish, the lobbyist in California. The newspapers of that state should have been printing that kind of thing for the last twenty years and none of them, when they had to pick up our yarn, could say the articles were "remarkably inaccurate" because they knew better. When last October Lester Velie went down to Kansas City and wrote the story of how Binaggio (a man with many connections in your state) was a hoodlum who had taken over the Democratic Party, he was far from being "remarkably inaccurate" because you now know what happened to Binaggio.*

On May 18th Sigma Delta Chi will present Velie with a bronze medallion for the Binaggio Story as the best magazine reporting in 1949. On the same day at a dinner at the Waldorf Astoria, this famous old professional newspaper fraternity will present to me a similar medallion for the best public service job in the magazine field in 1949 by reason of the Samish story and our series, "Terror in Our Cities." The judges are newspaper editors.

Senator Kefauver, chairman of the new crime investigating committee of the U.S. Senate, took time to compliment Schendel personally for his article on Illinois gambling.

You simply can't look at this on a personal basis, Adlai, in the face of all these factors. It would not have been necessary for you to send your state police out on belated raids and to take a critical blow from the Chicago Tribune if you had done the job you said you would do. The really important thing is to keep faith with the people. That is your strength. Green let the state get out of hand. Don't do that.

I could imagine Stevenson's reaction to Ruppel's advice about running the state of Illinois. It must have blown out all the fuses in the mansion. And, later in conversation when the governor commented petulantly to me:

"I don't see why local governments should expect the state to step in on problems like that."

..... it was all I could do to keep from replying bluntly:

"Don't tell me. Tell Ruppel."

I never told Stevenson about the correspondence from Ruppel and I found it extremely interesting that later accounts of this period in Stevenson's administration, as reported by historians and writers, made no mention of Ruppel's role in the matter. None at all.

---

* Charles Binaggio was shot to death by rival gangsters in his headquarters at the First District Democratic Club on Kansas City's North Side.

Vice-President Alben Barkley and *Adlai Stevenson* dedicating the new *Franklin Life Insurance Building* in *Springfield* in 1949.

Adlai Stevenson's brother-in-law, Ernest Ives, and John Dreiske of the Chicago Times, Springfield, 1950.

CHAPTER FIVE

The Lull Before . . .

I was intrigued by Stevenson's brother-in-law, Ernest Ives, the minute I laid eyes on him. He bowed in such a courtly manner at our introduction and kissed my hand. None of the newsmen ever kissed my hand. Besides, he sounded just like Herbert Marshall—sort of world-weary and travel worn— and he kept dropping references to places in Europe and his country estate in Southern Pines, North Carolina. I was charmed.

For some reason, *Chicago Daily News* reporter Charley Cleveland was not with us when the press first met Ives at a mansion get-together and nobody bothered to introduce them later.

One hot afternoon we were sitting around the pressroom in the statehouse when the phone rang with an invitation to drop by the mansion for mint juleps. It sounded like a good idea as we didn't have anything better to do. When we arrived, Ives was in the sun room officiating over the juleps, making quite a polished production of frosting the glasses, mixing the drinks and going into great detail about whether or not to bruise the mint. He was impeccable in a crisp white linen suit, white shoes and expensive cuff links, as he presided over all. It was quite different from the pressroom where the booze was kept in a filing case and you mixed your own drinks.

Charley sat there staring at Ives over his mint julep and not saying a word until Ives excused himself and left the room to get the governor. Then he turned to us and said dryly:

"I wonder where the hell Adlai dug that one up. He looks like he just came in from shooting a tiger!"

That remark ruined Ives for me thereafter. Whenever I ran into him, I kept seeing a pith helmet on his head. But I would have been disillusioned sooner or later. The governor's brother-in-law was not as egalitarian as I had thought. On the crowded closing night of the legislative session when space was at a premium, he had ordered a section of the public gallery roped off to provide room for him and his socialite friends so they could view the antics of the legislators. One of the newsmen got wind of this, however, and raised hell about it and the ropes came down like the walls of Jericho. There was never any inference that Stevenson had known about this, however, or the press probably would have had a field day over it.

Ives was married to Stevenson's older sister, Elizabeth, whose nickname was "Buffie" and who made her debut in Washington in 1918. In fact, we were told, she had been presented at the Court of St. James, whatever that meant to anybody. She had married Ives in 1926 when he was secretary of the American embassy in Constantinople.

Ernest and Buffie seemed to have ventured into a strange new world there in Springfield and didn't quite know what to make of us. We didn't know what to make of them, either. Buffie was a gregarious woman who strongly resembled her brother in looks as she flew around the mansion being the official hostess. She didn't greet you at the door—she swooped down on you with an air so effervescent that you could see champagne bubbles popping out of her ears, but God knows she was terribly devoted to Adlai, which was a refreshing change from his ex-wife Ellen, who had already started going around making uncomplimentary pronouncements about him.

During this desultory "off session" year, Stevenson's news conferences were few. Usually he held them in the mansion in his basement office. He had a large Dalmation named King Arthur (but called Artie) who sprawled at his feet growling occasionally at us as we scribbled away. Stevenson thought it was funny.

"He's accustomed to the wide open spaces," he told us.

"He's a transplant from Libertyville and I'm afraid he'll just never make the grade as a city dog."

Every now and then, Artie would slip out of the mansion and roam around Springfield getting himself thoroughly lost. Once he wandered into the Office of Price Stabilization building, leaped into an elevator and terrorized the passengers, all of whom got off hastily at the next floor. Somebody finally recognized him and called the mansion so they could send a state police officer to take Artie home.

Stevenson couldn't resist issuing an official statement about Artie.

"Dogs take on man's best ways," he said. "Artie's loyalty is unquestioned but when the master is away Artie becomes lonely and takes to running around the neighborhood covering the same total area he was accustomed to exploring on the farm. Artie's disregard of the city ordinance that forbids such vagabonding brings phone calls from neighbors. You see, most everyone knows Artie. He gets around a lot more than I do. In fact, when I go walking with him it's amazing how many greet us with, 'Hello, Artie.' However, he is a source of embarrassment to the police and to me. After all, a governor's dog may not have to be above suspicion but he should at least try to obey the law. His confined life here is not according to his nature, so we all try to make allowances."

Unless some of the Chicago political editors happened to be in Springfield on special assignment during "off session" years, the governor's news conferences were limited to the managers of the three news service bureaus, one or two local news reporters and, on occasion, a visiting journalist— usually from Washington or New York—who was studying the habits of the natives in the Midwest. Not much evolved from question-and-answer sessions because of the peculiar nature of news services, a facet of journalism not generally known by a public of newspaper readers who often wonder why the papers print what they do.

At that time, International News Service was the last of the "colorful human interest" wires supplying dailies and weeklies throughout the world. On an extremely limited budget (compared to United Press and Associated Press), more pains were taken with unique news features than with an attempt to provide full news coverage. INS doted on the "box" (a very brief item of human interest); the "sidebar" (a side story playing up an angle of a main story); and the personally by-lined (but ghostwritten) article by somebody in the news.

They were pretty blase about it, too. If some man hacked up his wife in my territory, I would get a bulletin message from the New York office to try for a by-liner from the husband, recounting the personal, thrilling story of how he hacked her up and why. Nothing was sacred. We INS people spent a great deal of time running around waving contracts at murderers, blind people who suddenly recovered their sight for no obvious reason, baseball players being sued for adultery, and anybody else who might be willing to part with the story of his life for a minimum sum and the glory of more publicity.

I once signed up a sheriff to tell about the gory slaughter of a woman and, as he told it:

"I found her head chopped off on the main floor and the rest of her was cut up and layin' around upstairs. At that point, I began to suspect foul play."

Under the circumstances, we had to develop a diversity of talents not required by the other two wire services plus the ability to outrun the competition. We got tickets to football games for clients, checked on hotel reservations, introduced our salesmen to prospective clients and even sometimes went out selling the service ourselves.

United Press was the one we had to beat—not Associated Press with its lumbering, methodical manner of plodding from one trivial point to another, employing all the imagination of an accountant in writing the news. United Press boasted of its ability to satisfy client requests by getting there "fustest with the mostest." They didn't always get there "rightest," though.

United Press also had its share of characters in Springfield. One of them, Don Chamberlain, a former war correspondent, operated the Springfield bureau as if he were still in the war zone. Everything was a bulletin. Everybody in his bureau had to step lively. Don, who was a portly, white-haired gentleman of fifty some years, could pound out a prep basketball roundup on the teletype with all the urgency of a wireless operator on a ship going down.

One day, when we were all summoned to the statehouse on a Saturday for an important announcement, we found most of the offices closed and no telephones available. Don frantically took off for his office at a gallop—down the steps of the capitol building, up three long blocks, around the corner, up a flight of stairs in the *Journal* building, down the hallway past the city room and around another corner where he skidded into the United Press office, shouted "BULLE-TIN!" and passed out.

It took his surprised staffers five minutes to bring him around to where he could tell them what the bulletin was.

Another aspect of Don's personality was his fanatical insistence on adhering to wire service code in teletype messages. We all had code books which were intended for saving time while transmitting as well as making it impossible for client editors and rival news services to decipher. The code consisted of words such as "AINA" for "Associated Press" and "ROCKS" which was the UP code for "INS" and "73's" which, in our books, meant "congratulations" and so on.

Combining words was another trick utilized to save wire space. "BUROS DOWNCOPY" meant to keep copy brief and stay off the wire as much as possible because a big story was breaking elsewhere. "UPDATE" meant to "BRING IT UP TO DATE" and "FOLO" was "follow through on another story related to the subject."

The list went on and on and, despite the so-called secrecy, we all knew how to read one another's code. Only Don insisted on pretending that they were carefully guarded secrets. Once, he left a hand scrawled message for a new reporter which read something like "ABBA DABBA CABBA UPGO 22 SKIDDOO UPDATE" and I had to decipher it for the poor kid who came rushing into our office for help. Don also felt it was part of the game to keep the opposition worried. He sometimes handed rolls of copy to a reporter with instructions to RUN past the Associated Press office as if carrying a hot story. AP couldn't have cared less.

Don was an ideal United Press employee, however—always on the alert for money-saving ideas. In the New York offices of all three wire services were employed accountants who had no interest in whether or not we got the news. We all had a vision of them as tall, thin men perched on stools, bent over desks, scratching away with quill pens by the light of candles. And all they knew of us was that we had spent $2.22 for a long distance telephone call about a coal mine explosion when, in their opinion, a letter would have done just as well. Or we had perhaps paid a stringer two dollars for a good exclusive when we could have sent him a jar of homemade piccallili and a thank-you note. When Don was after a story, any expenses he ran up were strictly incidental to the goal—but after the heat died down, he became very, very economical in an effort to appease New York.

One day he was sitting in his office, idly watching the pigeons strutting around outside on the flat rooftop adjoining the building, when an idea came to him. The more he thought about it, the more feasible it seemed. Why not train some carrier pigeons to deliver the news stories to the bureau? They were inexpensive, they didn't eat much, and they could be housed in little coops on the rooftop. The pigeons could be delivered to United Press correspondents throughout the state, who would write up the news story, put it in a band around a pigeon's leg and turn the bird free to fly back to Don's bureau in Springfield. He could open the window onto the roof, crawl out and get the pigeon and presto! A news story without paying telephone or telegraph charges! The New York office would be very pleased, Don felt, as he swung back to his typewriter and batted out a letter to them outlining his proposal.

A few days later, back came the answer. The New York bureau manager had written:

Dear Don:
    We've got an even better idea! Why not use parrots instead of pigeons? Then they could just tell you the story!

This unfeeling reply didn't bother Don as much, however, as the day he rushed to the teletype with one of his inevitable bulletins and, in his hurry, tripped over the electric cord, unplugging the machine. After crawling around finding the plug and poking it into the socket again, he tapped out a message to Chicago explaining what had happened and adding:

"SUGGEST REPEAT LAST STORY TO UPDATE ME."

Back came the teletype operator's reply:

"SUGGEST UP-PICK BIG FEET."

Associated Press people, on the other hand, never did things like this. They just went along covering everything in a very statistical manner, whether anybody wanted it covered or not, and their bureaus were about as exhilarating as a mortuary. They aimed to satisfy every little client out in the hinterlands, no matter what.

Under these circumstances, unless Stevenson dropped a blockbuster on us (which he didn't), we always listened politely to his routine announcements, jotted down a few notes, and then launched into our own peculiar requests. I frequently passed the time making up my shopping list or writing letters. Until I explained news procedures to Stevenson, he was clearly baffled as to why the Associated Press man spent so much time wanting to know what he thought about a bridge being refurbished over a small stream in an obscure downstate county.

"They have a client paper in that county," I told him after the conference, "and the paper has asked them to find out about possible state funding for the bridge."

As for United Press's insistence on a quote about the benefits of prep basketball—well, prep basketball was very big in Illinois, and more than likely, some client sports editor had requested that one for inclusion in a column.

"What's your angle?" Stevenson asked me.

"We're against vivisection and for dogs," I told him. "It's a long-time policy of William Randolph Hearst because of Irene Castle, who is a friend of Marion Davies, who is a friend of his. That's why I did a story on your dog, Artie, a while ago—because the Chicago *Herald-American*, which is a Hearst paper, requested it. And whenever Irene Castle comes here to Springfield to fight vivisection bills, I have to follow her around and write about her. So I don't have much time for you unless you do something terribly controversial."

Stevenson didn't think it was funny when I made a joking remark about the angles of the daily newspapers—something about how everybody in the pressroom could ghostwrite for everybody else because we knew what axe the individual newspaper was grinding. In short, we all knew how to slant.

There was more than average interest in the writing profession in Stevenson's family, of course. His oldest son, Adlai Ewing Stevenson III, served a stint one summer on the *Illinois State Register* in Springfield, during which his most frustrating problem was identifying himself on the telephone and then trying to convince the caller that he really was Adlai Stevenson. He finally solved the problem by changing to "A. E. Stevenson."

Although the governor took time out for a vacation now and then with his three sons and he played a little golf and tennis, he spent most of his time buried in work at the mansion. Entertainment there was sparse. Aside from the mint julep get-together, there were only a few informal press dinners from time to time, during which the entree consisted usually of something like meat loaf with tomato sauce and we sat around discussing politics and the upcoming legislative session. Another evening, Stevenson joined us for a poker party at the home of United Press man Don Chamberlain, and he played poker about as well as he played golf.

His tennis improved some that summer. He added William McCormick Blair, Jr., to his staff as appointment secretary. If Ernest Ives always looked like he just came in from shooting a tiger, Bill was a walking ad for "Tennis, anyone?" He even got Stevenson into the city tennis doubles competition—which they lost.

Bill was thirty-four years old and had had no previous governmental or political experience. A tall, darkly good-looking man possessed of a sardonic wit, his chief value to Stevenson was that of a trusted aide. Whatever the job paid, he didn't need the money. His father was a first cousin of the

Chicago Tribune's irascible old Col. Robert R. McCormick, and some of the money in the family came from the Cyrus McCormick reaper fortune.

Bill was a graduate of Groton and Stanford and had been in the China-Burma-India Theatre during World War II. He had an A.B. from Stanford and an LL.B. from the University of Virginia. In 1947 he was admitted to the Illinois bar, after which he joined the Chicago firm of Wilson & McIlvaine as an associate. I don't know when or where he met Stevenson but, from the start, I had the impression that he was probably closer to the governor than anybody else on the staff. He was a likeable sort but, politically speaking, theirs was a strange alliance considering Bill's Republican ancestry.

Stevenson had learned a hard lesson from his first bout with the legislature and obviously wasn't anxious for more of the same treatment. With the 1951 session approaching, he began expanding his staff to include people he thought could be of practical help and not just supply loyalty and admiration.

One of his additions was Carl McGowan, a dour-looking, forty-year-old former law professor, who was named the governor's legal advisor, succeeding Walter Schaefer, who was appointed to the State Supreme Court. Carl was quite able, but he had the personality of a porcupine whenever we approached him about anything and seemed to feel that what the governor did was no business of the public. Some years later, he became Judge of the U.S. Court of Appeals in Chicago, which seemed appropriate to me.

Stevenson made an exceptionally good appointment to the Illinois Liquor Commission, although we probably didn't appreciate him at the time. He was Willard Wirtz, who went on from that job to wind up eventually as U.S. Secretary of Labor under President Lyndon Johnson.

And, of course, he had Ed Day, who started out as an administrative assistant and in 1950 became Illinois Insurance Director, and a genial, likeable public relations man named Bill Flanagan, who had had United Press experience and was conversant with the problems besetting the news force but not able to do much about them. Don Hyndman, a former Associated Press man and a holdover from the Dwight Green administration, was an administrative assistant, and a young fellow named Larry Irwin acted as administrative assistant in charge of patronage. Dick Nelson, who had been active in the Young Democrats, filled in as another administrative assistant. (The title covered a lot and meant anything anybody wanted it to mean.)

We thought that one big plus which Stevenson had was the former *Chicago Sun* political editor, Jim Mulroy, who had the unenviable job of dealing with the various legislators, finding out what they wanted and talking up passable trades on this and that. It was a legitimate undertaking and one necessary in the world of politics, but it required a tough-mindedness in the face of so much frustration. Jim had worked hard on Stevenson's campaign, and he seemed to enjoy his new status in Springfield. It was easy to see why. He told me that he learned of the *Sun* merger with the *Times* only when he came into his office one morning to find somebody else at his desk.

He may have been exaggerating, but this was the start of an era in which newsmen all over the country were finding themselves literally run out of their offices in the wake of mergers and sellouts. (It may have been that the people who bought them out subscribed to the French theory of the guillotine in which it is considered more humane not to notify the victim of his execution date but to grab him suddenly, drag him quickly to the site, thrust his head under the blade and—ZAP!)

Mulroy had risen from cub reporter to Pulitzer Prize winner to editor. Then—ZAP! Now he was back in the running in his new job with Stevenson. One Sunday he invited some of us news people out to the house he and his wife had just bought and, after a few drinks, we wound up in his kitchen watching with deep interest as he demonstrated his garbage disposer, a novelty in that year. Only a person on a news salary could comprehend the delight with which Mulroy reveled in a garbage disposer.

For all our "walking with the great and near great," we were not in a well-paid profession, and the era of the fifties was only beginning to usher in the first wave of a more prosperous way of life. We had our pride, though, as Dreiske demonstrated once when he leveled off at a doctor who made the mistake of asking him, "How's the newspaper racket?"

"Do I ask you how's the doctor racket?" he stormed. "What makes you think the newspaper business is a racket?"

If it had been a racket, we would have been better off financially. When Dreiske showed up one day driving a brand new car, it was the talk of the pressroom. We all piled in and rode with him to a catfish joint in Beardstown just to give the car a good workout on the highway. Then we had to walk around it, admire the wonderful features that John pointed out to us and agree that it was a marvelous buy.

He spent much time prowling around it, polishing off a mark here and there, when he had it parked on the state-house grounds. And I shall never forget the day he showed up late at a governor's press conference and asked Stevenson plaintively:

"Can't the state do something about all these pigeons that keep shitting on my new car?"

It was understandable that Jim Mulroy's garbage disposer would take second place only to Dreiske's car. It was a sign of affluence, a status symbol.

Stevenson's relations with the press improved somewhat this second year in office, but probably only because the pace was slow and there was little to get mad at each other about. There was one incident involving him and the newsmen which will always stand out for me, however. The preceding December, we had been more saddened than we wanted to let on to outsiders by the death of old Charley Wheeler of the *Chicago News*. We had all gone to the funeral in Chicago and then up to a *Tribune* reporter's home in Waukegan for drinks and, at that time, had discussed some kind of something to do in Charley's memory. Something appropriate.

Shortly after the first of the year, as vice president of the Illinois Legislative Correspondents Association, I received a copy of a letter from Charley Cleveland to Charles Whalen, who was Associated Press manager in Springfield and also treasurer of our association:

> Brother Whalen:
> At the express order of one John Dreiske, grand exalted ruler (until comes the revolution) of the Illinois Legislative Correspondents Association:
> Flowers were sent to the funeral in the name of the association.
> Enclosed is said bill which, by request of above mentioned grand exalted ruler, is to be paid for out of said association treasury.
> Would appreciate your letting me know when the money is sent off so that I may again wander through the 19th ward where said florist establishment is established.
> (Signed) Charley
> 14th Assistant Junior Vice President
> in Charge of the We-Hate-Dreiske
> Subcommittee
>
> P.S. An idea—how about hanging a picture of Charley Wheeler in the pressroom or something like that?

We all liked the idea. The result was that we invited Stevenson to join Chicago's Mayor Martin H. Kennelly in a little ceremony on the night of June 29 in the pressroom honoring our late co-worker. We had a good photograph of Charley Wheeler, which we had framed with the inscription "He Was a Reporter" and hung on the wall. To the ceremony we also invited the leaders of the House and Senate and Charley's granddaughter, Nancy, and his son, Marsh.

Perhaps the reason I remember so vividly what happened is that it was a most difficult assignment for Stevenson to take on. It was a solemn occasion in which he was surrounded by a bevy of news editors not noted for solemnity and touchy as a boil. It seemed impossible to say the right thing and it was almost excruciating to watch the people involved bumble awkwardly through in such an intimate little gathering.

After Kennelly's prosaic remarks, Stevenson stepped forward, looked around somewhat hesitantly and then began talking in a conversational tone, as if addressing just one person instead of a room full of people. He had once attended a meeting in Chicago, he said, when the main speaker was the governor from another state. Midway in his talk, the speaker had faltered and then had collapsed. In the confusion that ensued, Stevenson recounted:

"I realized that somebody should call for an ambulance immediately and I rushed to locate a telephone. In the hallway was a sign with an arrow pointing—to a telephone, yes, but unfortunately it was in the ladies' 'powder room.' Back and forth I paced for a few seconds. Should I? How serious was the emergency? Finally, my mind made up, I squared my shoulders as best as these shoulders would square, flung open the door and courageously marched in."

He paused.

"And there on the phone was Charley Wheeler calling the story in to his paper!"

We loved it. Charley would have loved it, too. And it was perhaps Stevenson's closest moment with the press. For a few minutes there, we were one in remembering a great old gentleman and honoring him—appropriately.

Springtime in Illinois was observed that year with another outburst of gangland warfare involving what was left of the old Shelton gang, which wasn't very much. After covering the story and filing it to Chicago, I rapped out a fake news story about the governor deciding to issue hunting licenses where Sheltons were concerned and sent it to him. Back came the response:

Dear Pat:
I have just read the best news story ever written in Springfield—"Hunting Licenses for Sheltons." I am sending it to the Director of Conservation, confident that he will prepare suitable rules and regulations to handle the applicants in an orderly manner, without danger of trampling or claustrophobia.

ADLAI: THE SPRINGFIELD YEARS

As a public official, I am deeply grateful for the stirring, penetrating, accurate way you have handled this major news break. INS should be proud.

> Sincerely yours,
> (signed) Adlai E. Stevenson

P.S. Perhaps licenses might be issued on a target practice contest at the State Fair—with a suitable admission fee, and appropriate handicaps for myopic politicians!

For my own part, the year was one of deep frustration at my inability to get a good job elsewhere. It was not that I disliked what I was doing. I simply felt that I wasn't really accomplishing much with my life and I certainly wasn't getting ahead. Discussing this with Stevenson one day, I mentioned to him that I had made a trip to Chicago to apply for a job with the Chicago Council on Foreign Relations. Shortly after, I was surprised to receive a carbon of a letter from Stevenson to Mrs. Quincy Wright, head of the Council, who had interviewed me.

Dear Louise:

Miss Patricia Milligan, Springfield correspondent for the International News Service, tells me that she has been talking to you about a job with the Council. She is a bright, alert, tough-minded gal, whom I have seen since I have been in Springfield at press conferences. I think she evidently feels thoroughly frustrated in her present work and would make a financial sacrifice to get out of this journalistic "dead-end."

I know nothing about what you have discussed or her personal circumstances, but I know she is able, industrious, humorous, and "conditioned" in a hard school in competition with bright boys on the way up the wire service ladder.

This is gratuitous.

> Yours,
> (signed) Adlai E. Stevenson

There was no job opening at the Council so I stayed in Springfield for the time being, but I appreciated his help in supplying a reference.

When not preoccupied with his work on the affairs of government, Stevenson spent much time writing his speeches. I covered many of them and started jotting down notes and stuffing them away. By that time, I had met quite a few men in positions of power, I had interviewed many of them for INS, and I was finding them shadows compared to Stevenson. It was like knowing two people in one—the gifted orator who could hold my attention in a crowd but who was a stranger in so many ways, and the very human, sensitive man who seemed to regard the orator critically and with some disparagement. I do not know where I got it, but one of the excerpts I scribbled down went:

> It has fallen to our lot as it did to the ancient Greeks in their time, and to the Romans in theirs, to make a unique contribution to human history.
>
> What is that contribution? I would say it was the realization of an idealist's dream of a free society in which hopes and aspirations once reserved for the few are the property of the many.
>
> The American system of public education is both the symbol and the means of our great contribution. To show us the way to this concept of democratic society is the aim of the teacher.

In October of that year the *Chicago Sun-Times* editorialized that: "Stevenson's public speeches show revealing flashes of real statesmanship and a broad outlook."

Of course, a part of the appeal Stevenson had for listeners consisted of his self-deprecatory remarks. Nothing is more charming in a person of exalted status than the occasional reference to human frailties, provided the frailties are minor (and even lovable) and provided it isn't overdone. Beneath those remarks of his burned as much untarnished ego as in any other individual of extraordinary talent. I never found this inconsistent with his achievements. The people put Stevenson on a pedestal in Illinois, regarding him in awe as something special and simultaneously insisting that "he's just a good old boy like us."

If Stevenson had been a "good old boy like us," he wouldn't have been governor. He liked to talk about the good life on the farm and going back to the earth and all that nostalgic drivel, but he wasn't talking about getting up before dawn and trudging out to the north forty to start a day's ploughing.

That Christmas, I joined another reporter, Milcie Lane of the Associated Press, in concocting a cornily written "Christmas Cantata" for Stevenson. It wasn't really funny but, like a family joke, consisted of slapstick humor based on knowing the characters involved and the inside story. We set new lyrics to currently popular songs, wove them into a plot featuring members of the legislature and the press, and bundled the whole works off to Bill Flanagan. Bill ran off mimeographed copies, selected the cast from among the governor's staff, and went into rehearsal.

On Christmas day at the mansion, our "Cantata" was presented as a surprise present to Stevenson. Despite the corn, he must have enjoyed it and I think he was pleased that we had thought of him. On the day after Christmas, he wrote a two-page letter thanking us and describing it as "an imperishable piece of Americana, combining the best in contemporary music, verse and political satire."

Musical background, he wrote, was provided by "a vast chorus of splendid voices ranging in age from 2-plus to 60-plus, some loaded with turkey, and some just loaded."

We were glad to know that he had enjoyed it. Ahead of him lay his next session of the legislature, the members of which were pawing the ground impatiently awaiting the confrontation.

CHAPTER SIX

"The 'Little Guy' Wants It"

During his first legislative session in 1949, Stevenson had gone up against a Republican Senate and a Democratic House and had come off badly. This time—1951—he faced a formidable all-Republican legislature licking its chops in anticipation of an even bloodier slaughter.

But this time he had something going for him in the very substantial personage of Democratic Sen. William J. Connors, a ruddy-faced, corpulent Irishman who got his degree in Political Science from the teeming, head-knocking wards and precincts of Chicago's near North Side. Bill had been a political boss for years and during the 1949 session, he didn't any more know what to make of Adlai Stevenson than Stevenson knew what to make of him. Sometimes he would just stare at Stevenson with an incredulous look on his face and then turn to us and shrug. The rest of the time he trudged heavily around, chomping on a cigar, shaking his head over what odd breed had come to inhabit the governor's mansion.

He was taciturn, blunt, gruff, earthy and not particularly interested in discussions of a philosophical nature. With a glass of whiskey in one hand and the inevitable cigar in the other, the canny old pro would listen, say not a word, size up the situation, figure out the odds and then proceed to deal.

"It ain't how much you know, Pat," he once told me, "it's what you do with it."

Stevenson was better educated (formally), better read, more extensively traveled, considerably more eloquent and certainly much more conversant in the world of wit and intellect. But Big Bill Connors knew how to wheeler-dealer a bill through the legislature, he knew where the bodies were buried, and he was a master of the delicate art of utilizing just the right tactic at the right time.

Stevenson had had it drilled into him all his life that you do certain things because they're the right things to do—the *morally* correct things. In his precision world, you tried to reason things out with yourself, consider the various possibilities, arrive at a decision, and then proceed to sell others on your position in much the same manner. You used logic— you exercised intellectual persuasion and psychology—you attempted to enlist help in the name of the common good.

Bill had a slightly different approach to the problem. In his book, there were guys who went along with you and guys who didn't want to. So you found out what the bad guys wanted and, if it was reasonable, you worked up a trade. Having done a lot of favors in the past, you had a lot of tabs you could call in. Give a little here, take a little there, patch this up, work that out—and if somebody absolutely refused to cooperate, well, a little political clout now and then never hurt anybody.

Stevenson badly wanted a bill passed to increase the state's gasoline tax from three to five cents a gallon in order to finance Illinois' public highway system. He planned to introduce a biennial budget of $1,300,000,000 which would involve no new taxes and he very much wanted the gas tax bill to go through. In fact, he pointed out during the session that if all the pending legislation involving bridges and roads were enacted, the state budget would be thrown out of balance by almost one hundred million dollars.

"This is a disturbing and dangerous approach to our highway problem," he said at a news conference which I covered. "Everyone recognizes that Illinois has too many 'political' roads as it is."

He was wrong about that. Not everybody recognized this. It was a long standing maxim of the legislators, who depended on the home folks and not on Adlai Stevenson for votes, that "there's always room for one more road." The building of roads (and statues) was a way of life, as far as they were concerned.

Stevenson's reaction simply wasn't the same as theirs to almost anything. He seemed to assume that some high motivation should be evident in everything they did, and he was never exactly inhibited about expressing his disapproval. (Although he did exhibit some signs of growing skepticism when I mentioned to him that a lawmaker had introduced a resolution to investigate state parks and he replied, dryly, "Why? Is one missing?")

At the opening of the session in January, he recommended legislation to prohibit the manufacture of gambling devices in Illinois and to compel tavern keepers to obey the anti-gambling laws. Under the law then in effect, the manufacture, sale or lease of gambling devices was prohibited only in counties in which military or naval posts were located, and Stevenson wanted no repeat of the Ruppel episode involving gambling.

When Democratic legislators James Gray (from East St. Louis) and Kent Lewis (from Robinson) introduced Stevenson's bills, the Republicans and one Democrat promptly sponsored a bill appropriating $50,000 to set up a so-called Little Kefauver Commission to investigate crime in Illinois.

Stevenson didn't fully understand what was happening until the Republican dominated Senate efficiency and economy committee recommended that his antigambling bills "do not pass." But his newly acquired political savvy was beginning to emerge.

When the "little Kefauver" bill was introduced, the governor had issued a statement that he welcomed a serious investigation of crime in Illinois by the state legislature, knowing full well that the Republicans simply intended to try to embarrass him with any disclosures they might make by emphasizing that these wrongdoings were occurring under his administration. At the time, the governor was careful to tell us at a news conference:

"I assume that we may now expect enthusiastic support from the legislative leaders of both parties of the legislation I recommended on January 3 to prohibit the manufacture of gambling devices in Illinois."

He was all set when the Republicans killed his bills. He exclaimed tartly:

"I am completely at a loss to understand this action or to see any justifiable basis for it! I am also struck by the fact that one of the members of the committee who opposed these bills is a sponsor of the bill to set up the so-called Little Kefauver Commission. I can only inquire—do the supporters of this legislative commission wish to get rid of crime in Illinois or merely to investigate it?"

Of course, the so-called West Side Bloc was particularly sensitive about any crime bills. Members of the Bloc regularly traded with downstate legislators, agreeing to vote for their bills in return for "anti" votes on crime legislation which applied mainly to the Chicago area. Rural politicians were happy to cooperate with the Bloc.

Their attitude, which was as fixed as the statue of Lincoln in front of the capitol building, was that anything concerning Chicago was of no interest to them except as a basis for bargaining. Criminal elements in Cook County could not possibly have the slightest influence on affairs in their own bailiwicks, as far as they were concerned. Each legislator operated on the basis of what would affect him vote-wise and always with reverential respect for the leading lobby groups who, in splendid, time-honored tradition throughout the years, fattened their campaign coffers. After every election in Illinois, some "Good Government" group or ambitious district attorney always demanded an investigation of "election frauds." The investigation was held, the publicity boosted somebody else along the trail to higher office, and nobody went to jail for payoffs, ballot box stuffing or voting long dead constituents. It was all so nicely nonpartisan. In fact, when this 1951 session convened, one of the first resolutions piously urged "an investigation of alleged fraudulent voting in Cook County."

Such cooperation between Democrats and Republicans was never understood by the public, who believed naively that the two parties were always locked in deadly battle. Except for individual power plays and grudges, there was a viselike adhesion between the forces which operated to shut

94

out the public—particularly when any third party attempted to get on the ballot. Republicans and Democrats toiled together many a night, checking validity of names on petitions presented to the secretary of state's office by third party personnel and, failing all else, conveniently "lost" the petitions until the date for certification had passed.

But, as Stevenson was finding out, come Lincoln's Birthday, the Republican officeholders and their relatives and payroll appointees dutifully laid a wreath on Lincoln's tomb and gave speeches blasting the Democrats—and on Jefferson's birthday, hordes of illiterate Democratic hacks rallied round at $25-a-plate dinners to extol the virtues of Jeffersonian Democracy and castigate the Republicans. There was more truth than humor to a remark made by Sen. Arthur Larson, a Chicago Republican, who was discussing a bill to raise salaries of legislators. At that time, a senator made $3,000 a year with take-home pay of about $2,452. Weekly expenses ran about $50, which was $10 more than the state paid. Larson summed it all up philosophically when he said that "the raise would certainly attract higher type men to the Senate."

Stevenson's nickel gas tax bill proposed allotting 40 percent of the increase to the state, 30 percent to cities, 22½ percent to counties and 7½ percent to townships. The three-cent gas tax in effect at the time split the take equally among the state, cities and counties.

In addition to Republican opposition, Stevenson faced a battle with members of his own party when a second gas tax bill was introduced by Sen. John Fribley, a Democrat from downstate Pana, and three other downstate senators. Fribley's bill would have channeled 37½ percent of the increased revenue to the state, 25 percent each to counties and cities, and 12½ percent to townships.

On the advice of his aides, Stevenson called in Bill Connors, who was minority whip of the Senate, for a conference on strategy, and when the incongruous two finished discussions, they had agreed on their battle plan, lined up their forces and prepared to charge. During the weeks following when the flak was flying, Connors acted as Stevenson's field marshal, dodging each burst with aplomb, maneuvering in the back rooms in little secret meetings before sessions, easing his huge girth into his chair in the Senate in time for the call to order for parliamentary procedure, then conferring with his own lieutenants in hotel rooms after sessions and girding for the new day's war of nerves. Whenever one of the legislators balked a bit, Bill would chomp on his cigar, glare at him and growl, "The little guy wants it." And during it all, "the little guy" stayed in the mansion as per their agreement, removed from the scene of battle in body but following it avidly through his legislative aides.

When it was all over, both the Republican opponents and the divisive Democratic group accepted surrender terms, Senate Bill 97 was passed, and in the press room we dubbed Bill Connors "Casey Jones" in honor of his skillful engineering of "Old 97" through the Senate, even though we had the wrong train number. We all felt that both Connors and Stevenson had proved something—we weren't sure just what, but it was the most fascinating partnership we had ever seen in action. As one of the newsmen put it: "They danced so well together—and we didn't even know they were engaged!"

It was a landmark for Adlai Stevenson in that politics had rubbed off onto him and he, in turn, had injected some of his philosophy into the motivation of that old in-fighter, Connors. From there on, we all noticed the mutual respect between the two men.

By the halfway mark of the session, action was pending on some nine hundred bills. A total of 364 bills had been introduced in the Senate and 560 in the House. Of this figure, nine Senate and seven House measures were passed. Stevenson had signed six of the House bills and six of the Senate bills and had vetoed two Senate bills. By way of contrast, a total of 1,133 bills had been introduced in the 1949 session and of these, 497 had become laws.

As usual, things began to get more than a little hectic, tempers became sensitive, nerves started crackling, mouths began to tighten, eyes sent off sparks, and normally gentle-mannered individuals pushed in front of page boys and slammed doors on little old ladies.

Dreiske got into his biennial battle. This time it was with State Rep. William G. Horsley, a Springfield Republican who took exception to one of John's columns and gave a speech on the floor of the House referring to John as "imbecilic and moronic." Horsley, who was a lanky lawyer, liked to get dressed up like Abraham Lincoln every February 12, put on a beard and go stand on the rear platform of a train at a Springfield depot and deliver Lincoln's farewell address when he left for Washington. John chose to retaliate for Horsley's insults by greeting him effusively whenever the two met in the hallway and congratulating him over and over on his oratorical ability. Horsley finally broke under the goading and offered to take off his spectacles and meet John outside the House chamber, but John declined.

"I'm a writer—not a fighter," he said disdainfully. "Besides, I might hit you in the mouth and then you couldn't put on your Lincoln beard for a while."

Then he walked off, leaving Horsley sputtering furiously.

We also suffered through another "dog bill" encounter during the session between Irene Castle Enzinger (for the dogs) and a number of legislators (against the dogs) involving a bill to provide more stray dogs for medical experimentation. Mrs. Enzinger's abrasive personality turned me off— at one point, she snapped at the legislators, "I am NOT a frustrated woman, as you may think! I've been married over and over!" But the legislators turned me off even more with their foolish barking and yapping whenever the bill came up for action. I noticed once that a number of school children were in the gallery on a tour of the statehouse in order to study their government firsthand—and none of them laughed.

A group of housewives got my vote when they marched into a committee hearing on legalizing the sale of colored margarine in Illinois. At the time, the dairy industries had lobbied legislation through prohibiting the sale of margarine in any form other than its natural pallid state. Busy housewives had to take time out to mix the margarine with a pellet of coloring, an arduous chore. The women got their bill out of the hostile committee by calling in the press, handing out bowls of margarine and packets of coloring to the startled men on the committee and telling them to start mixing. Under the wicked eyes of the news cameras, the men folded and voted the bill out "do pass."

But the real fireworks of the session, next to the governor's gas tax bill, exploded on the "anti-Red" bill.

There was an interesting prologue to this. Earlier in Stevenson's term, a resolution had been adopted by the legislators, calling for an investigation of subversive activities at the University of Chicago. When the hearings were held, there was much interest throughout the state—and our Illinois Legislative Correspondents Association was deluged with requests from visiting newsmen to use the facilities of our pressroom in the statehouse. One of the persons writing in for permission was a girl who identified herself as a representative of the *Daily Worker*. We agreed with John Dreiske that she was entitled to the same privileges granted any other news representative and she was so notified. However, she failed to show up and we forgot all about her.

When the hearings started in the House chambers, the spectators gallery was crowded with jostling, muttering, glaring young people—mostly students, I gathered, and a scattering of bearded individuals wearing horn rimmed glasses and puffing on pipes. I couldn't decide whether they were professors, Communists or men who just wanted to be interviewed.

The legislators in charge of the investigation were very pleased with themselves as the press photographers went around flashing pictures, and the reporters went around interviewing everybody who would say anything, no matter who or what he was. The Associated Press bureau chief, Charlie Whalen, stepped out of the press box once to talk to someone and was stopped by a little old lady who tried to press a five dollar bill in his hand.

"What's this for?" he asked, startled.

"To help fight the Communists," she breathed fervently.

He handed the money back.

"I can't take this," he said.

"Why not?" she retorted impatiently. "Everybody else does!"

We were still laughing about it when Dreiske passed me a note informing me that I was being given the eye by a long, skinny man leaning against a pillar just outside the House floor and that I might be overlooking a good matrimonial prospect. Dreiske notified me regularly of such possibilities on grounds that I didn't know what was best for myself and needed his help. This time, he had really outdone himself.

My "admirer" was Ichabod Crane with large ears, a bowl haircut and a long nose. He definitely was ogling me—which was hardly a compliment to me, as I told John, inasmuch as I was the only female in the press box, and besides, if I couldn't do better than that on my own, I was a lost cause. As the hearing progressed, Ichabod's interest in me grew to the extent that he began to follow me around the statehouse in an awkward, loping gait which attracted even more attention and embarrassed me considerably.

He would hang around outside the pressroom, pick up my trail when I emerged and follow me back to the press box. He even shadowed me when I went to the rest room. Finally, in desperation, I picked up the phone, called the local FBI office and reported the fellow.

The agent who took my call was puzzled at first—then the light dawned.

"Oh!" he said. "Is he tall—kind of gawky—walks like a farmer in a cow pasture? Picks 'em up and puts 'em down?"

"Yes," I said.

"He used to be with us," the agent said sadly. "I don't know why he's following you around, but he's harmless."

Piqued at this, I told Dreiske, who immediately charged right up to Ichabod demanding to know why he was making such a nuisance of himself. Dreiske came back to the press room in a high state of indignation.

"That jackass!" he exclaimed. "Somebody told him there was a girl here reporting for the *Daily Worker* and he thought it was you!'

We never did find out why he was following me around on his own unless he was what one might term a "free lance" espionage agent. The woods were full of them at "Red bill" hearings. Dreiske turned up another one subsequently when he was approached by a man seeking press credentials as a reporter for the *St. Louis Post-Dispatch.*

"You work for the *Post-Dispatch,* eh?" Dreiske said, with a sadistic gleam in his eye.

"Yes."

"Been there long?"

"Oh, a couple of years."

"Well," said Dreiske, "I want you to meet somebody here."

He led the "reporter" to a desk occupied by *St. Louis Post-Dispatch* newsman Roy Harris.

"Roy," he said pleasantly, "I'd like you to meet somebody who's been working with you for two years."

The startled "newsman" broke and ran and we never saw him again.

The real explosion at the hearings came, however, not during the testimony in the House chambers, but after hours one night at a press party in the ballroom of the Leland Hotel. Both the Hearst newspapers and the *Chicago Tribune* were backing the Communist inquiry into the University of Chicago and were lending considerable support editorially to two individuals who had been retained to pursue the investigation—Dr. J. B. Matthews and Howard Rushmore.

Matthews, a towering, gray-haired Methodist minister, described himself vaguely as being "from the South" and immediately took exception to our questions about the "Dr." title. Was this, we wanted to know, a degree in medicine, philosophy, education, theology or what? Or, as Dreiske put it:

"Do you cut people up? Or did you just go to college for a long time?"

Matthews had been research director for the old Dies House Un-American Activities Committee, he said, and he had uncontrovertible evidence that more than two thousand college professors throughout the country had records of participation in Communist fronts. He described New York as the center of Communist leadership, with Chicago as a close second. And he was prepared to introduce documentary proof at the hearings that the University of Chicago was a a hotbed of homosexuality.

All this he told us in an impromptu interview in the press room on the opening day of the hearings. At the time, he had in tow Howard Rushmore, a rather diffident reporter for the *New York Journal-American* (a Hearst paper) who apparently was the paper's expert on communism. Rushmore did not appear to relish his role and stayed pretty much to himself. But Matthews was a different type of rooster.

That night at a Leland Hotel press party, he swaggered in with a *Chicago Tribune* official just as we were finishing a buffet style dinner. Most of us were wandering around with after-dinner drinks when he charged up to the bar, ordered what obviously was not nearly his first bourbon of the evening, and stood there unsteadily gazing around until his bleary eye fell on me.

Lurching over, he began a rambling and incoherent diatribe on the subject of homosexual college professors, and as I kept backing away from his hot breath I soon found myself backed up to the wall.

"Tomorrow at the hearing," he reiterated, "I am going to produce sensational evidence that most of the teachers at the University of Chicago are queers and you—(he poked a shaking finger at me) will have a sensational story for Hearst!"

"What's the evidence?" I asked him.

"My evidence!" he shot back. "And you can run it word for word on the INS wires and Hearst will give you a big fat raise!"

One of the newsmen laughed. I was sensitive enough about working for Hearst under those circumstances, and my temper flared.

"I'm not running anything that isn't thoroughly documented," I snapped. "There are libel laws, you know."

At most, I had expected Matthews to argue with me and was completely unprepared when he suddenly burst into full-blown rage so explosive that the other news reporters fell silent in awe. The man was literally beside himself—not only from drink but from some emotional turmoil which was rather frightening. I shrank back against the wall and got ready to duck in case he should swing at me in his paroxysm of fury.

"You'll run what I say and you'll run it in full!!!!**&%#% ——Who do you think you are telling me you won't run my evidence???)***(&*%%&&** —— Do you know who I am??? ((*(&&¢¢¢——I'll have your job—you're in your last job with Hearst—I'll see to that tomorrow!!!!"

One of the newsmen pushed in between us facing Matthews while another signaled the surprised *Chicago Tribune* official to hustle his friend out of there. Everyone was very indignant. And solicitous. The more they kept telling me how nervy I was, the more I forgot about how scared I had been, and I began to enjoy it. By the time the party was over, I was sailing around feeling very much like a heroine instead of someone stupid enough to try reasoning with a drunk.

It wasn't until the next morning that the impact of Matthews' remarks hit me. I had no doubt that he could get me fired and I needed the job.

In the pressroom that afternoon, just before the hearings were scheduled to open, I was talking with some of the newsmen about my possible fate when Pete Akers, who was managing editor of the *Chicago Sun-Times,* approached me. Pete had not been at the party the night before but he had heard about it.

"If that guy gets you fired," he said, "you've got a job on the *Sun-Times.*"

For two years I had tried unsuccessfully to get a job on the *Sun-Times* on the basis of my experience and ability. Now I was getting a bona fide offer based on being fired for fighting with a drunk at a party. I couldn't have cared less. At that moment, all I wanted was to get sacked. And at that precise moment, while visions of a brand new job with lots of fun in Chicago's night life circles were dancing through my head, into the press room marched the redoubtable Dr. J. B. Matthews, graying head held high, bloodshot eyes fixing me with piercing stare and hand held forth somewhat shakily.

"Apparently, I had a little too much last night," he said,

"and they tell me I was a bit rude. Shall we let bygones be bygones?"

What could I do? In dismay, I shook his hand while the prospect of my exciting new job slipped below the horizon. Pete was sitting right there watching.

"But you don't have to worry about libel," Matthews went on importantly. "Anything said at that hearing is privileged. So you can run my evidence word for word on the INS wire."

I thought he was going to pat me on the head condescendingly.

"You know," he pontificated on, "when a professor associates with a homosexual, he's open to suspicion himself. So I wouldn't waste any sympathy on those people. They should know better."

At this point, Pete spoke up.

"Guilt by association, you mean?"

Matthews shrugged.

"Call it what you like," he said.

"Yeah, well, that's very interesting," Pete responded, nodding his head. "Gives me an idea for my next editorial."

Matthews, who hadn't the slightest idea who Pete was, perked up.

"What is it?"

"I think," said Pete, swinging back to his typewriter, "I'm going to write an editorial about you entitled 'Guilt By Intoxication'."

Two days later, the entire investigation of the University of Chicago collapsed, the committee members scattered and everybody went home. Neither Matthews nor Rushmore was seen in the area again, although I read rather frequently in the years to come about the meanderings of Matthews through various state legislatures and before committees of this and that. He served briefly on the U.S. Senate investigations subcommittee of Sen. Joseph R. McCarthy and claimed he was forced to leave the job by "bigots" following publication of an article in a national magazine in which he charged more than seven thousand Protestant clergymen with comprising the largest single group supporting Communist apparatus.

He went on to describe New York as the center of Communist leadership, with Southern California second as a Red stronghold in the United States. He didn't say anything about Springfield.

Unlike the early hearing, however, the one scheduled in Stevenson's second legislative year did not attract such a flamboyant audience. Perhaps in 1951 even the public was wearying of interminable investigations of Communist activities. However, the matter posed a very real problem to Stevenson, who would be forced to sign into law or veto the results of this particular inquiry, inasmuch as it hinged on a bill introduced by Sen. Paul W. Broyles, a Republican from Mt. Vernon, and Sen. Robert J. Young, Jr., a Democrat from Hurst. It was Broyles who had headed the 1949 legislative investigation employing Matthews.

Under the provisions of the bill, a fine of up to $20,000 and one-to-twenty years imprisonment could be imposed for attempting to overthrow the government, advocating its overthrow or contributing to the support of any subversive organization. A fine of up to $5,000 or one-to-five years in prison could be levied for being a member of any subversive organization. In addition, the bill required that candidates for office and nearly all public employees sign loyalty affidavits. Persons convicted under the act would lose their right to run for office and to vote.

Most of the fireworks went off in the House where the bill was sent after passing the Senate 34 to 15 on May 1. Everybody wanted to deliver a stirring speech on patriotism, particularly since the American Legion was a prominent sponsor of the legislation. Veterans', church and women's groups were among the chief supporters of the bill which had been patterned after Maryland's Ober Law, and legislative support from within came strongest from downstate Republicans, while most Cook County Democrats were opposed. House floor leaders for the bill were Representatives John P. Meyer (a Republican from Danville) and Clyde L. Choate (a Democrat from Anna who was a Congressional Medal of Honor winner from World War II).

Meyer proclaimed from the floor during the debate that: "A Communist is a Communist whether he lives in Springfield, Chicago, Moscow or Seoul!"

Everybody applauded except the Civil Rights people glowering from the sidelines. Arguing against the bill was Rep. Robert E. Romano, a Chicago Democrat, who insisted that Illinois already had all the laws needed to combat communism, fascism and all other isms.

"Communism, like any other political belief, is an idea!" Romano exclaimed. "If it is treasonable to stand up and speak for an idea, then I may be called treasonable!"

Another Democrat, Rep. William Pierce of Rockford, also opposed the bill, warning that "This House will be setting a precedent it will be ashamed of sooner or later." Then he added, "Frankly, this is a bad bill."

But after all the shouting was over, the bill was passed by a vote of 87 to 42 and went to Governor Stevenson for final action. I knew what a spot he was on. I also knew what he was going to do. He had told me in advance, and he was so casual about it that it was obvious he had never entertained a thought about compromising his principles for the sake of political expediency. He vetoed it.

Stevenson had problems in other areas, too. The West Side Bloc legislators were in evidence much more strongly during this session of the General Assembly than they had been earlier. They adopted the practice of appearing at the sessions attired in Hawaiian shirts, somewhat the way a neighborhood gang of boys goes in for leather jackets. At a mansion party one evening, Stevenson was obviously startled when a West Side Bloc-er whipped out a bird whistle and began blowing it at intervals for no apparent reason.

Another legislator in that group was more belligerent, particularly after he had had a belt or two. Early in the session, he would prowl from table to table at the Leland Tavern, drink in hand, accosting other legislators, leering at the women, asking them loudly, "Will you or won't you, baby?" and roaring, "When I drink, everybody drinks!"

(That last opinion of his wouldn't have gotten him anywhere at the mansion.)

Not all the West Side Bloc-ers were like that. Senator Libonati was so friendly that it was difficult to remember at times that he openly admitted owing his law school education to the beneficence of Al Capone, who had more than a casual interest in bringing up criminal lawyers the way they should go. Libonati went around generously offering free tickets to stage shows in Chicago "or whatever you have in mind when you come up there," and he bragged once to me that he had helped a legislator (whom he declined to identify) beat the rap on a rape case.* Libonati went on to Congress later.

With the close of the session, Stevenson was in a much happier frame of mind than he had been for some time. He seemed more relaxed, more confident of himself. At a luncheon at the mansion one day, he admitted to me that he was beginning to suspect that he had always had a predilection for politics but that it had taken a few victories to bring it out. I got the impression that he was pleased at his performance with the legislature the second time around.

Shortly before Christmas of that year, I decided to put into effect my own ruling against accepting the annual expensive gifts sent to news people by politicians and lobbyists. I had given thought to this in previous years when the Chanel No. Five and the Teachers Highland Creme and the $50 bills had rolled in and nobody else had thought a thing of it. This time I wrote polite little notes to the donors informing them that INS had put this policy into effect (I didn't have the nerve to say it was my idea).

Back came a letter from Stevenson:

Dear Pat:

I am sorry I "pushed" you. And as for imbuing anyone with a crusading spirit—well, I am glad it happened, but I have always suspected you of being already highly spirited in that direction. So I refuse to accept the blame.

* Tagge once casually introduced the senator to a dignified, retired businessman with the helpful information "If you ever get charged with rape, he can help you."

Anyway, you are right, but I suspect the Christmas ham will arrive all the same. If you spurn it, send it back and we will eat it here some night.

Sincerely yours,
(signed) Adlai E. Stevenson
Governor

It irked me that he had seen right through me and I was prepared to set him back by returning the ham—just to show him I meant what I said. But what irked me even more was that the ham never arrived!

All I got from him was a Christmas card illustrated with a sketch of the wrought iron railing on the south porch of Lincoln's home, atop which were perched two cardinals flanking the words:

Governor Adlai E. Stevenson
wishes you a
MERRY CHRISTMAS!

CHAPTER SEVEN

1951 — No Vintage Year

So far, Stevenson's administration had been untouched by scandal (except for the gambling incident), not a bad record for an "amateur" politician. Considering his disinclination to become involved in "petty gossip," he was fantastically lucky, too!

During this third year of his term, serious trouble began to erupt in the area of race relations. After a summer vacation trip to Wyoming with his sons, he returned to Springfield to face a race riot in Cicero, touched off when a Negro family moved into the neighborhood.

To his credit, he acted decisively, calling out the National Guard and making it clear that he would not tolerate the rioting. There was no improvement in race relations, however, and at that time Stevenson never said anything to me to indicate his awareness of the depth of America's race problem. In fairness, neither did any other public official.

Housing constituted the hard core of segregation in Illinois. Although there were a few black legislators (there had to be from all-black areas), they were hardly exemplary representatives of their race. One of them regularly made speeches in favor of a state Fair Employment Practices Commission— then went around trading votes to make certain his fellow legislators voted it down. An FEPC was the last thing he wanted, inasmuch as this constituted his sole campaign issue. Without it, he had nothing on which to run. (He had a counterpart in the white ranks who consistently introduced legislation to enforce prohibition and frequently was too drunk to appear on the floor to vote.)

There were no blacks in top jobs under Stevenson and, I am sure, nobody wondered why. But there were no blacks in top jobs anywhere in the country in those years, nor was there any recognition of a problem. Just sporadic riots presaging the agony to come.

Stevenson's patronizing attitude toward women never changed, either. He was perplexed when I resented one of his favorite stories, which he repeated at banquets so often that I suspect he did it to bother me. The story was an old one in which two women were arrested for crusading for women's rights, and whenever Stevenson delivered the punch line "Pray to God—SHE will help!" he always glanced over somewhat impishly in my direction.

(Another of his favorite stories which I enjoyed more was one in which he and a Russian diplomat were arguing over some matter which had been snarled up in red tape.

(Stevenson would relate with much relish:

("I said to him 'but you people are the ones who are behind!' Whereupon, he reared up, looked me right in the eye and said, 'Mr. Stevenson, I did not come here to discuss OUR behind but YOUR behind!' ")

Stevenson didn't always practice what he preached. He was, for example, an ardent and vocal advocate of the inherent dignity of the human, but his actions in some instances struck me as being contradictory. Perhaps I expected too much of him in that day and age.

I noticed this not only in his failure to appoint Negroes and women to responsible positions but also in his veto of an anti-public housing bill passed by the Senate. The legislation in effect, provided that public housing developments be approved by a referendum among the neighbors in the area. Should the residents vote against the development, none could be started there.

My quarrel with Stevenson's veto was not that I approved of the bill as it stood but that I objected to the fact that he failed to point out the moral responsibility of our more affluent citizens to pay more equitable wages to minorities so that they could afford their own adequate housing. I also wondered if Stevenson would react thus if public housing projects were planned adjacent to his farm in Libertyville.

While his veto ostensibly upheld the rights of the poor, it

seemed to me more a reiteration of the ruling group's dictum that the poor we shall have with us always —— but near somebody else and not us.

In his veto message, he wrote:

"This bill would retard the construction of urgently needed homes. Each new project, each new plan, each new site would require a separate interpretation to the voters. Experience has shown that every additional control affixed to the administration of the program has been at the expense of the results.

"If the principle of this bill were sound, why should not we require a referendum within two miles* of each proposed new school in the city of Chicago before it could be built? And should not the state then require a referendum within two miles of any airport? Should the residents immediately adjacent to Congress Street have to approve its construction? Should we require a referendum around each particular area where a park is to be located? Should the surrounding neighborhood vote on whether to have new police and fire stations, hospitals, streetcar barns, a library, a tuberculosis sanitarium, a post office? Would the sponsors of this principle want each neighborhood to vote on whether people from other neighborhoods could use its parks and libraries?

"It would be a dangerous doctrine to say that a public improvement, which by law and judicial interpretation is for a public purpose, is now of concern only to the people in the immediate surrounding neighborhood. Who is to determine where the limit of interest ends? If this theory were to prevail, why two miles? Why, one might ask, should it not be one house, or one block, or one hundred yards? To what extent would the sponsors of this bill carry the notion that public improvements are only for the benefit, and therefore only the concern, of people in the immediate vicinity. Moreover, if this type of legislation were to become law in respect to low cost housing, on what logical basis could the same

* The bill stipulated that in Chicago the residents of a ward any part of which was within two miles of any part of such a project could vote on the issue.

111

right be withheld from the residents of areas to be redeveloped by private enterprise?

"I think it unwise, indeed dangerous, to substitute government by referendum for government by representation even in this limited area. Nor can I approve such a transparent device to scuttle the low cost housing program and reverse the long-established public policy of the state."

I always considered this one of the most telling veto messages issued by Stevenson, one which said to me that he was far from being an all-out liberal and was, in fact, quite conservative when faced with an innovative departure from traditional attitudes.

My opinions in no way detracted from my growing admiration for Stevenson, the statesman. His veto message on the bill to define subversive organizations, make them illegal, force candidates for public office to sign loyalty oaths, and so on, was superb and one which required considerable courage. Stevenson likened the legislation to Russian tactics in creating an atmosphere of suspicion and distrust and asserted that it was unrealistic to assume that such bills would be effective in combating Communist treachery in America.

"Basically," he wrote, "the effect of this legislation, then, will be less the detection of subversives and more the intimidation of honest citizens. But we cannot suppress thought and expression and preserve the freedoms guaranteed by the Bill of Rights. That is our dilemma. In time of danger we seek to protect ourselves from sedition, but in doing so we imperil the very freedoms we seek to protect, just as we did in the evil atmosphere of the alien and sedition laws of John Adams' administration and just as Britain did during the Napoleonic era. To resolve the dilemma, we will all agree that in the last analysis the Republic must be protected at all costs, or there will be no freedoms to preserve or even regain. But if better means of protection already exist, then surely we should not further imperil the strength of freedom in search of illusory safety.

"We must fight traitors with laws. We already have the laws. We must fight falsehood and evil ideas with truth and

112

better ideas. We have them in plenty. But we must not confuse the two. Laws infringing our rights and intimidating unoffending persons without enlarging our security will neither catch subversives nor win converts to our better ideas. And in the long run, evil ideas can be counteracted and conquered, not by laws, but only by better ideas."

After all the flak thrown at him over the Alger Hiss deposition, *that* took guts.

Stevenson's handling of the scandals which surfaced that year also reflected a high degree of executive ability and a talent for acting decisively except possibly in the case involving his trusted aide, Jim Mulroy. Had Jim committed an illegal act, there is no doubt that Stevenson would have had no reservations but there was never even a charge of illegality.

The story broke in the fall of 1951 after Chicago newsmen went down a list of names supplied by Sen. Estes Kefauver's Crime Committee in connection with Chicago Downs, a harness racing association operating at Sportsman's Park in Cicero.

During the 1949 session of the legislature, a bill legalizing Chicago Downs had been passed unanimously. The newsmen checking the Senate Crime Committee list discovered that several legislators, Chicago politicians and state employees had gotten in on the ground floor, buying stock for only ten cents a share. In just a few months time after passage of the bill, the stock jumped to $1.75 per share, and according to the records, Mulroy had paid $100 for a thousand shares and had received a return of $1,750, a right tidy profit in anybody's book. As things turned out, he had bought the stock at the invitation of one Paul "The Meat's A-Cookin' " Powell.

There was nothing illegal in Jim's stock purchase, but it was generally felt that race track promoters don't cut people in on exorbitant profits without a reason. Particularly promoters connected with Sportsman's Park, long associated with the old Capone gang and the Chicago syndicate. Some of the other Chicago Downs stockholders, for example, were Hugo Bennett, listed as auditor of the park, who once loaned eighty thousand dollars to a syndicate leader named Paul "The Waiter" Ricca. Another was William H. Johnston, Jr., son of the operator of Sportsman's Park and a man described by Kefauver's committee as having had "a long career of close association with Chicago racketeers and the Capone gang."

Both the *Chicago News* and the *Sun-Times,* staunch supporters of Stevenson, were quick to denounce Mulroy's involvement with the association. One of the newsmen, Clem Lane, who was city editor of the *News,* said tartly, "I suppose public officials will go on operating on the sordid principle that if it's legal, it's honest." Public criticism of Mulroy was harsh.

Despite the outcry, Stevenson maintained that his aide had been guilty only of bad judgment. The story broke in late August and the pressure on Stevenson to demand Mulroy's resignation was intense. On October 29, Jim submitted a letter in which he said:

"I have considered most carefully, and with a full realization of your motive, our conversation of some weeks ago. There is no doubt in my mind that you believe that I would penalize myself by remaining in my present capacity." He then went on to say that continuing in his job might impair his health.

Mulroy's health had not been good and he had, in fact, been hospitalized several times. Once when I was hospitalized with a strep throat, he had been a patient just down the hall, suffering from shingles. However, there was no doubt in my mind or anybody else's that Stevenson had finally given in to the pressure and had asked Jim to resign. When he accepted the resignation the governor issued a statement quoting from a letter he had sent Jim in reply:

"I hardly need to add to what I have often said, but let me take this occasion to again tell you of my personal appreciation for the devotion you have given your work and me."

It was a tragic finale to a newspaperman's career. A few months later, Jim died.

The cigarette tax scandal was entirely different. There had been attempts before to forge cigarette tax stamps, but the

114

first indication of a major gang operation came early in 1951. Counterfeiters working in conjunction with cigarette wholesalers stole several tax meter machines, made new dies and plates and used the stolen machines to counterfeit the tax stamps. In all, the state lost about one million dollars in revenue in the brief period in which the racket operated.

When reports of the racket filtered down to state officials in Springfield, Stevenson quietly appointed a friend of his, Ben W. Heineman, to head an investigation of the matter. Heineman was a Chicago corporation lawyer who was named assistant attorney general by Stevenson and given a free hand in conducting the probe.

For several months the secret squad moved around in Chicago, buying cigarettes and learning to spot the phony stamps. When they were ready, they moved in on November 27, staging raids on ten wholesale firms in the Chicago area. Even the Chicago police knew nothing about the matter until the raids occurred.

As a result, the following spring saw the conviction and imprisonment of the president of one of the firms and charges filed against a number of others. Licenses of the raided establishments were revoked, three state revenue department employees were fired and a third resigned.

Still another scandal broke when Stevenson learned to his chagrin that his appointment of Frank Annunzio, a Chicago politician and CIO labor leader, as his director of labor, was a bad choice. Just the previous year, Annunzio had become the Democratic ward committeeman in the First Ward of Chicago and when Stevenson heard about it, he gave Annunzio the choice of his state job or his ward job. The governor rightly contended that members of his cabinet should not engage actively in politics, no matter which party was involved. Annunzio quit the ward job, which was an unfortunate choice from Stevenson's viewpoint.

It seems that the labor director had been a partner in an insurance agency with John D'Arco, a West Side Bloc man and state legislator who helped kill Stevenson's "con con" and "crime commission" bills.

115

Annunzio and D'Arco called their agency "Anco, Inc." and set themselves up as president and vice-president, respectively. Another officer of the firm was a man who had been convicted of vote fraud back in 1928 and who had had close ties with the Capone gang.

When a Chicago ward committeeman named Charles Gross was assassinated, the subsequent investigation disclosed the association between Annunzio and D'Arco and, even though Annunzio had sold his stock in "Anco, Inc." and had resigned his presidency at about the time he had resigned his ward job, the heat was on. Ten days after the disclosure, Annunzio handed in his resignation to Stevenson, who accepted it without delay and, I am sure, with a great sense of relief.

Stevenson pointed out that Annunzio had done nothing illegal, which was true, but once again, he said that it was "a question of judgment." Although he had said the same about Jim Mulroy, it was obvious that there was no regret on Stevenson's part in accepting the resignation in this case.

As to why Stevenson had made such a dubious appointment in the first place—the CIO had supported him strongly in 1948 in his bid for governor.

The worst scandal by far in the Stevenson administration was the famous "horsemeat racket." The story did not emerge until 1952 but had its roots in the preceding summer when Stevenson's Agriculture Director Roy Yung reported rumors that horsemeat was being sold as hamburger to unsuspecting Illinoisans. Under Stevenson's instruction, Yung assigned his superintendent of foods and dairies, Charles Wray, to investigate the rumors. Wray did so and reported back that he was unable to find any evidence to back up the rumors.

A few months later I was working away in the news bureau when I received a phone call from Jack Heil, public relations director of the Federal Office of Price Stabilization, inviting me to a news conference. Jack, who was a friend of mine, added the intriguing suggestion that I skip lunch that day, which mystified me.

When the disclosure was made at the conference that much of the hamburger we had eaten during the past few months had been "horseburger," we all felt a trifle ill . . . except the United Press reporter who said he had eaten horsemeat during World War II and didn't mind it.

"It's all in your mind," he said confidently. "Horsemeat is as clean as beef or pork."

"Not this horsemeat," the OPS official said grimly. "A great deal of it had been condemned as unfit for dog food."

The UP man suddenly looked bilious.

"How can we tell if we ate some of it?" he asked pathetically.

"How often do you eat hamburger?"

"Oh, once or twice a week."

"You ate it."

The OPS official went on to explain that the meat was doctored with a chemical nicknamed "dynamite" to give it a cherry red color and help disguise the rotten parts.

A Chicagoan named Joe Siciliano was placed under arrest, at which time he came up with the plaintive assertion:

"Gee, you'd think I ground up Man o' War!"

Of course, state meat inspectors were involved. They had to be. Under Carl McGowan's direction, Agriculture Director Yung had summoned them to a weekend meeting in Springfield in the Agriculture Department offices at the state fairgrounds, and by the end of the two-day session (which involved lie detector tests), it was announced to the press that Charles Wray had admitted taking $3,500 from Siciliano. Wray had been Stevenson's personal choice for his job as superintendent of foods and dairies and there had never been a blemish on the man's reputation until then. In fact, Wray's family had won the honor of "typical farm family of Illinois" at the state fair just the preceding year.

After Wray had signed a statement, Yung fired him. Later, Wray was indicted and a dozen or so state inspectors were fired or suspended. (Subsequently, Wray repudiated his statement to McGowan and his case was thrown out of court on a technicality.)

The horsemeat scandal hurt Stevenson's administration despite the fast work he had authorized after the OPS disclosure. His failure in the case had been the failure, also, of Yung to assign an independent outside investigator to the case.

Moreover, the Chicago syndicate was deeply involved in the racket which produced millions of dollars in illegal profit while the people of Illinois—the honest little taxpayers and hard workers and good citizens—were direct victims of the sordid affair. To my mind, this was another example of Stevenson's disinclination to get involved directly in what he considered petty talk. He accepted Yung's report that Wray had discovered nothing when a little common sense should have told him that people investigating themselves aren't too likely to incriminate themselves.

I couldn't imagine old Sen. Bill Connors doing that. But a lot of the people around Stevenson appeared to be incredibly naive when it came to human nature. I never found out on what basis they judged people but whenever they became overly enthusiastic about somebody or something, I got suspicious.

Stevenson's relations with the press this third year of his term were no better than they had been all along, and I despaired of ever convincing him that his deeply suspicious attitude toward newspeople wasn't helping any. I didn't understand his reasoning, although I understood fully why he told one of his office aides (who told me) that I was the "smartest" of all the news corps covering him in Springfield. It was flattering, but he didn't really mean that I was the smartest—what he meant was that I was the only one who listened to him!

CHAPTER EIGHT

But They Liked Ike

On January 20, 1952, Stevenson flew with Bill Blair to New York City to address the National Urban League. With uncanny luck, *Time* magazine had scheduled a cover story on Stevenson, not knowing that President Truman would ask the governor to meet with him in Washington after the League speech. There was, of course, no hint in Springfield (or anywhere else, for that matter) that Truman was casting about for a successor.

Of course, the visit between the two men at Blair House, which was the temporary White House at the time, caused a flurry of publicity and speculation among the press. Stevenson's speech on civil rights before the Urban League dinner received much favorable mention in the New York papers. Also, the *Atlantic Monthly* was out with a lengthy article about the Illinois governor.

The suddenly erupting national publicity caught us by surprise back in Illinois, but apparently Truman's proposition caught Adlai by surprise, too, because he had just announced that he would be a candidate for reelection as governor. By the end of January, however, the *New York Times* was "columnizing" like fury and the rest of the press was beginning to enjoy a field day with the subject.

In the meantime, Stevenson returned to his official duties in Illinois and to repeated denials that he would be a candidate for the Democratic presidential nomination—denials which, at that time, obviously were true. But when Truman announced on March 31 that he would not be a candidate for reelection, the heat of full-blown publicity was turned onto Stevenson so blazingly that he finally issued an official statement sixteen days later:

> I have repeatedly said that I was a candidate for governor of Illinois and had no other ambition. To this I must now add that in view of my prior commitment to run for governor and my desire and the desire of many who have given me their help and confidence in our unfinished work in Illinois, I could not accept the nomination for any other office this summer.

Nobody believed him.

There were other coincidental news incidents which emphasized the situation. A few months earlier, CBS newsman Eric Sevareid had visited Springfield and, at the suggestion of *Chicago Sun-Times* editor Pete Akers, had looked me up. Over a drink at the Leland Tavern, I filled him in on Stevenson so that he could do a radio newscast about him. Sevareid, who was then chief of the CBS Washington office, told me he had met the governor before and had been greatly impressed. His radio newscast added to the rumor that Stevenson might be a presidential candidate.

In addition, I was surprised to receive a letter on January 31 from Louis Ruppel informing me that two men from *Collier's* magazine—Howard Cohn, an associate editor, and Marvin Koner, a photographer, would be in Springfield within the week to do a feature on Stevenson:

> I have told them to look you up and to ask your cooperation out of which I think you might make a small bob. I'd prefer not to have it noised about but we plan it as a constructive piece about the governor. I had a pleasant talk with Adlai today. Howard will fill you in on arrival.

When I called Stevenson about it, he went on guard right away.

"That depends upon how you define constructive," he said coldly. "Constructive for whom?"

As it turned out, the *Collier's* article was so pro-Stevenson that it was hard to believe that the same editor had belted him out of the ring a couple of years earlier.

All this publicity kept us busy in Springfield, writing and rewriting stories about the governor for dissemination throughout the nation. No longer was he just a local boy. The more Stevenson copy I fed into our teletypes, the more the New York and Chicago offices demanded. I told Stevenson that it was almost as bad as Lincoln's Day every year when I had to dredge up "new slants" on old Lincoln stories.

"It's hard to come up with something new," I told him, "on somebody who's been dead for a long time."

"Are you implying a correlation there?" Stevenson asked me dryly.

During that period, I never asked him directly about his feeling regarding the presidency, even in a general way. At that point, it seemed unreal to me, anyhow, and I suspect he shared the feeling. We did talk about his attitude toward his job as governor and out of all our conversation, what remained with me was his light-hearted remark that:

"Maybe I was born at the wrong time. During the thirties, people were blaming their troubles on the bankers. Now they're blaming the politicians. The hell of it is, I was in the banking business then and I'm in politics now."

I assumed he meant his years as a lawyer when he worked with banks. In one of my feature yarns about him, I included this story and also mentioned that he often worked late alone at the mansion and that anybody calling the number probably would get him personally. After my story was printed, Stevenson asked me somewhat acidly if I would not run any more items like that. It seems he was being inundated with late phone calls—one of which was from a man who, against the background sounds of a jukebox and clink of glasses, shouted to his buddies:

"I got Adlai!! I win the bet!"

Another of his callers, he said, was a small boy who blurted:

"I'm not going back to school ever again and you can't make me and neither can President Truman!"

Stevenson said he could hear in the background the parents hissing:

"Hang up! Hang up!"

On March 28, Phil Reed of our New York INS office sent me a letter marked "Urgent" which read:

> We have a tip from the editor of Harper's magazine that Stevenson may get into the presidential ring some time early in April. It is pretty vague but something that you may want to keep an eye on. So please watch developments there in Springfield.

I couldn't resist forwarding this to Stevenson with a note on it: "If you see a face at the window, for God's sake, don't shoot!"

Back came his reply—a scrawled "Not that face—but look out for a kiss! AES."

Under all the kidding around, however, was a disturbed feeling on my part—particularly when President Truman announced that he would not be a candidate for reelection—that things were happening too rapidly to assess properly. And perhaps too easily.

At a time when intelligent political reporters were staying close to Springfield, I took a six-weeks leave of absence to make a leisurely vacation trip to the West Coast, during which time the Democrats held their national convention in Chicago, and I returned to Springfield to find a presidential candidate in the mansion, newsmen and women crowding into the little capital city, and an INS man from Washington assigned full-time to Stevenson.

Perhaps Stevenson summed up my own feelings best when he replied to a brief letter of congratulations which I sent him:

> August 19, 1952
> Dear Pat:
>
> I was deeply touched and pleased by your letter. You were thoughtful to write and it was most heartening to hear from my "old" friends.
>
> I sometimes long for the good old days when Artie and I

could come and go at will. Unhappily, the "iron curtain" has descended, but I hope that does not mean I shall lose touch with you.

Sincerely yours,

(signed) Adlai E. Stevenson

Thereafter, as Stevenson's days in Springfield neared their end, I had to face up to the fact that I did not care to continue there. It seemed simply that the time to leave was at hand and would never be so right again.

My only contact with the presidential campaign occurred when I filled in during an emergency on an interview with Richard Nixon during a stopover in Springfield just prior to his "little dog Checkers" speech.

I did play a part in introducing a visiting journalist to the Stevenson entourage—a very pretty twenty-one-year-old Miss Yvonne Blumenthal, who was with the publicity department of the Hotel Del Prado in Mexico City, and who had arranged to visit Springfield in hopes of writing an article on Stevenson for the Mexico City newspapers.

Miss Blumenthal showed up in my office to ask if I could help her in obtaining press credentials. She was a member of the Mexican Press and the Foreign Correspondents Association of Mexico, and had studied journalism at Trinity University in San Antonio, Texas. She spoke four languages fluently, she told me, was seriously interested in both journalism and politics, and would do her very best not to be a nuisance if I could just manage to slip her into one of Stevenson's news conferences.

Miss Blumenthal also happened to be dazzling! She had shining auburn hair, lovely dark eyes, and a smile that would send any man crashing through the ceiling. Moreover, as she talked so earnestly about her career, she seemed completely unaware that she was a knockout.

"Do you think you could help me?" she asked. "I would be so grateful."

It was no trouble at all. After filling her in on what I knew about Stevenson, I took her over to his press headquarters

123

to introduce her to the newsmen. On the way, we ran into Stevenson's brother-in-law, Ernest Ives, whose eyes popped out a city block at the sight of Miss Blumenthal, and who bowed, presented her with a Stevenson pin and did an "about face" to join us.

As I had suspected, Miss Blumenthal was not even asked for her press credentials. They asked for mine—but not hers. Leaving her surrounded by newsmen jostling one another aside in their eagerness to assist her in her chosen career, I couldn't help pondering a bit about how true talent will always shine through—and wishing I had some of that kind, too.

A Springfield columnist present at the news conference which Miss Blumenthal covered was so taken with her that he devoted his entire column to "the young ambassador of good will from Mexico" whom he described as a "satisfying eyeful in a red dress, a full-skirted peacock-blue, green and white print over plain green, sashed with a wide green cummerbund." After going into further detail about her jewelry, he asserted that "the cool, exotic colors set off her lovely auburn hair and dark eyes perfectly" and "her musical accent was delightful."

Then he really "waxed eloquent." His prose went on:

"This is but another episode in the marvelous drama being enacted here by top-flight journalists who are drawing vivid word pictures of Governor Stevenson for millions of newspaper and magazine readers, with Springfield, rich in history and Lincoln lore, as the colorful background."

If the news about Stevenson from Springfield was sparse that day, Miss Blumenthal was the reason. Shortly after, she wrote me from Mexico City thanking me for my help and enclosing clips of her stories—in Spanish. What with one thing and another, I didn't get around to having somebody translate them for me until years later when I stumbled across them. Out of curiosity, I looked up a friend who spoke Spanish and who read to me, among other things, the fact that I was quoted as saying:

"Stevenson is so modest a man that he does not even have a private telephone in his residence!"

124

Stevenson conceding the 1952 election.

Adlai would have loved that!

Just a day before my departure from Springfield, I called the mansion and told one of Stevenson's secretaries that I had resigned my job and wanted to have her pass along my good-bye inasmuch as I knew how busy he was with his campaign. It seemed the easiest way to handle it.

Almost immediately, however, I received a letter from him which was forwarded to me from my former news service office:

Oct. 12, 1952

Dear Pat:

I was told that you are shaking the dust of Springfield from your winsome feet. I hope you are doing the right thing. At my age, one gets a little conservative and cautious, I suppose, but I am confident that you will find firm ground for those feet wherever you are.

My best wishes and happy memories go with you. I shall never forget your professional good will and personal friendship during our years together here in Springfield. Nor shall I forget the cantata!

Best luck.

Sincerely yours,
(signed) Adlai E. Stevenson

I was in Denver working on a temporary job for a public relations agency when he stood up before a crowd of tearful campaign supporters in the ballroom of the Leland Hotel in Springfield and conceded the victory to Dwight Eisenhower. When I wrote him, I felt there was so much ahead for him that I made a point of emphasizing that this was a temporary setback. He responded on December 15:

Dear Pat:

You were sweet to write me and I am mortified that your letter of November 7 has only now come to my attention.

I don't regret the campaign—except for the disappointment

125

of so many dear and loyal friends including yourself. But I am distressed about Illinois and all the toil and sweat of these past years in Springfield when you were such a comfort to me. I wish the story of those years could be written some time, but I am a little tired and indifferent at the moment!

I hope all goes well with you and I am grateful indeed for your lovely letter.

Yours always,
(signed) Adlai E. Stevenson

CHAPTER NINE

Stevenson and the Nathan Leopold Story

When I left Springfield in 1952, I took with me an unpublished article on a bizarre set of circumstances involving Stevenson, a convicted thrill killer and Professor Albert Einstein.

For several years, I had been fascinated by the case of Nathan Leopold, who at the age of nineteen, took part in the murder of a young boy in Chicago in 1924 "just for the thrill of it." It is doubtful that Stevenson ever met Leopold, but when both were children, their families vacationed at Charlevoix in Michigan, which was a favorite summer spot for well-to-do Chicagoans.

When the Nathan Leopold case broke again during Stevenson's first year as governor, I was interested enough to begin a project of research which wound off and on through almost three years, led me into a visiting room in Stateville Penitentiary just outside Joliet and later put me in touch with Dr. Einstein. The aspects of the case and the ironic crossing of paths were so nearly unbelievable that I decided to write an article and then, for good reason, buried all the material unpublished in my files.

The story started for me in 1949 when Stevenson issued a statement cutting Leopold's ninety-nine-year sentence to eighty-five years as a reward for participating in malaria experiments during World War II. Stevenson's action, which was the unanimous recommendation of the state parole board, meant that Leopold could be paroled on January 9, 1953. At that time, he would have finished twenty-eight years and four months in prison.

None of us in the news world had known about the malaria experiments which had produced a new, highly effective

127

drug called pentaquine. It was termed the first curative drug for malaria and was used on U.S. troops in the South Pacific.

Leopold had volunteered, along with some four hundred inmates, to be used as a "guinea pig" in the development of the drug, had contracted malaria and had been treated successfully. All the convicts who took part in the tests were given special consideration, even though no promises had been made in advance, but Leopold was such a notorious figure that an immediate outcry of indignation erupted, much of which was directed at Stevenson, who had merely followed the board's recommendation. The governor was unperturbed.

In part, his statement read:

"I have received the report of the Board of Pardons in the case of Nathan Leopold and have concluded to reduce his sentence from ninety-nine to eighty-five years.

"This decision has been most difficult. While the Board of Pardons unanimously favors a commutation of sentence, it has not been able to agree as to the amount of reduction.

"Under a sentence of eighty-five years he will be required to serve a total of forty-three years and nine months and would be discharged on the commuted sentence on June 11, 1968. He will become eligible to apply for parole in January 1953. If such application is made, the parole board will consider his case at that time. This action today has no bearing on any possible decision to be made by the board in the future."

Stevenson concluded that:

"The commutation in this case was recommended, and is being made, pursuant to a program to reward prisoners who voluntarily risked their lives in malaria experiments for the armed services."

And he added a postscript:

"Pursuant to suggestions from Governor Green early in 1947, the parole board has given special consideration to prisoners who voluntarily participated in the malaria research program. It is the conclusion of the board, and I concur, that Nathan Leopold is also entitled to this consideration."

Knowing the case would be coming up again, I decided to dig into the background in order to be prepared, and I began to while away my spare time in the newspaper files and utilize every opportunity to quiz the members of the parole board on their ideas and opinions. (Most of them were cautiously noncommittal, but one of them surprised me by insisting that he had voted against his better judgment. "Leopold's getting special privileges in the penitentiary," he told me. "They're trying to cover this up but I happen to know that his money's playing a big part in the treatment he gets there.")

Leopold was an unusual individual from the day of his birth on November 19, 1904. He was the precocious and pampered son of a Chicago millionaire box manufacturer who had catered to the boy's every wish. At the age of eighteen, he was graduated from the University of Chicago law school.

His friend, Dickie Loeb, also considered a near genius, was the son of a Sears Roebuck vice president. Dickie was eighteen and Leopold nineteen when they decided to pull off the "perfect crime" for no apparent reason other than that they wanted to prove they could do it. On May 21, 1924 the two young men were cruising around Chicago's South Side in a rented car looking for an appropriate victim. They spotted luckless fourteen-year-old Bobby Franks, who was the son of a multimillionaire watch manufacturer and whom they knew slightly. It was no trick at all to lure Bobby into the car.

According to all the research I was able to do, nobody ever proved which of the young men actually slugged Bobby over the head, but it was generally believed to have been Loeb. (Shortly after their arrest, each accused the other.) Following an abortive attempt by Leopold and Loeb to force a $10,000 ransom payment from the Franks family, the boy's nude body was found stuffed into a culvert.

Two newsmen from the *Chicago Daily News* were prowling around the culvert afterwards and stumbled across Leopold's spectacles where they had fallen from his pocket. Subsequently, they traced to Leopold the ownership of a typewriter used for the ransom notes. The newsmen, who

129

were awarded the 1925 Pulitzer Prize for their work on the case, were Alvin Goldstein, Sr., and James Mulroy.

Now, in 1949, Mulroy had popped up again in the case as one of Stevenson's aides. He withdrew from any participation in the matter in order to avoid any possibility of being accused of prejudice.

Actually, the public throughout the nation was so incensed by the vicious crime that Leopold and Loeb escaped the gallows only because of the brilliant plea of their attorney, the famed Clarence Darrow, who was smart enough to forego a jury trial (which almost undoubtedly would have netted the death penalty) and seek mercy instead from Judge John R. Caverly in Cook County Criminal Court.

Under Illinois law, the court could have sentenced the two young men to be hanged or to be imprisoned for any period from fourteen years to life. They received life for murder and ninety-nine years for kidnapping, a sentence passed after Darrow's impassioned plea which gave him the opportunity to expound his own opposition to capital punishment and his theory that the youths were as much a tragedy of wealth as other criminals were a tragedy of poverty.

This was not exactly the easiest theory to expound in 1924, particularly when Loeb and Leopold showed no signs at all of remorse and explained almost cheerfully that Bobby's murder was an experiment evolved from their studies of the German philosopher, Frederick Nietzche, regarding the writer's theory of "supermen" who could murder without sense of guilt.

Darrow did not contend that Loeb and Leopold were insane, but he did claim that they were mentally ill, which touched off a wave of argument throughout the country as to "what's the difference?"

Jacob Franks, the father of the slain boy, was in the courtroom when Judge Caverly passed sentence, and his comments as reported by the press afterwards interested me greatly.

"There should be an eye for an eye, a tooth for a tooth," Franks was quoted as saying. "I have faith enough in the people of Chicago to know that these two boys never again will walk the streets free men."

Darrow himself had said in his plea:

"I will be honest with this court as I have tried to be from the beginning. I know that these boys are not fit to be at large."

But he had added:

"I believe they will not be until they pass through the next stage of life, at forty-five or fifty. Whether they will be then, I cannot tell. I am sure of this; that I will not be here to help them. So far as I am concerned, it is over."

Judge Caverly, however, had made it quite clear that in passing sentence, he did not want the boys ever admitted to parole.

"The court feels it is proper," he had said, "to add a final word concerning the effect of the parole law upon the punishment of these defendants. In the case of such atrocious crimes, it is entirely within the discretion of the department of public welfare never to admit these defendants to parole. To such a policy, the court urges them strictly to adhere. If this course is persevered in, the punishment of these defendants will both satisfy the ends of justice and safeguard the interests of society."

Loeb was killed by a fellow inmate in 1936 who claimed that Dickie had propositioned him, thus prompting the often quoted newspaper story which began with macabre humor:

"Dickie Loeb ended his sentence today with a proposition."

But when the parole board held its first hearing on the malaria volunteers, a statement by the prosecuting attorney in the case, Robert E. Crowe, was read into the record:

"In malice, premeditation and deliberation, the crime of these defendants is unequaled in the criminal history of the state. I desire to emphasize most emphatically the absolute necessity from the standpoint of the safety of society that these degenerate murderers be imprisoned for the entire period of their natural lives."

At this hearing, one witness made a plea for Leopold. He was a Northwestern University professor and criminologist named W. F. Byron, who asked that Leopold be returned to society "so the world may gain by his great brain." Professor Byron, who termed Leopold "highly egocentric" at the start of his prison term, told the board:

"Then it was 'Nate Leopold, the boy genius.' Then it was 'Nate Leopold who committed the perfect crime imperfectly.' Since then there has been a growth in his sense of responsibility. That wonderful brain of his could work on cancer research or sleeping sickness. In my opinion, he is a good risk and society would gain from his freedom."

So Adlai Stevenson waded through all the testimony and background and arrived at his own decision and that was that—for a time. He probably thought I was a bit of a bore about the Leopold case, but was too polite to say so whenever I got on the subject.

In 1949, of course, we had no way of foreseeing that the 1953 parole hearing date for Leopold would see Stevenson gone from the scene. So I continued my research, poring over old files and doing a little writing and rewriting and then, in the summer of 1952, I forgot about the story when I got caught up in Stevenson's first presidential venture. It wasn't until after his nomination at the convention in midsummer that I remembered that Leopold was due for his first parole hearing within a few weeks. This, I decided, would be the most opportune time to try to interview him—when all the other reporters were preoccupied with politics.

It was easy to do. One of the parole board members suggested I contact Warden Joseph Ragen directly, and my request was taken in to Leopold who agreed to the interview. (He set forth one condition, however, which was that we not discuss the crime and that our conversation center on his life in prison.)

When I arrived at Stateville Penitentiary outside Joliet, I was subjected to a thorough search by a matron and then marched through an "electric eye" doorway. My purse was upended and the matron temporarily confiscated a swizzle stick left over from the preceding evening's martini ("this could be used as a sharp stick into an eye," she explained) and a package of Tums ("anything edible could contain poison").

Next, I was escorted across a courtyard and admitted to the administration building, where I was scheduled for an interview with Warden Ragen. His secretary ushered me into his office and after introductions were exchanged, she carefully left the door open while returning to her desk. I noticed this.

"Oh, it's a routine precaution," he explained. "Sometimes women relatives of prisoners have been known to try a little blackmail in the form of screaming rape, so I instructed her to leave the door open whenever I have a woman visitor."

He acted as if it were a mite humorous—but I noticed he still left the door open.

"What is Leopold like now?" I asked him curiously.

Ragen shrugged.

"Nothing to distinguish him in looks," he smiled. "He's the richest man in the penitentiary, of course, but everybody looks pretty much alike in here, you know."

"I wonder how much money he has."

"I don't know," Ragen replied thoughtfully. "Seems to me that his father left him fifty thousand or so in a trust fund and that was way back in the twenties, so there's plenty. Not that it does him any good in here."

Without identifying my source, I told Ragen what the parole board member had said about Leopold's receiving special favors. He frowned.

"Not true. Every man gets the same shake in here. I couldn't run a penitentiary on favoritism if I wanted to. How long do you suppose it would be before a riot broke out? I'm not saying that some of our guards aren't doling out favors now and then behind my back. I know human nature. But nothing big is going on."

For a while we discussed penitentiaries and how to run them. I was impressed with Ragen's ideas.

"The ball and chain are out," he said, "but don't get the notion that I'm soft. This is a maximum security institution and we don't take chances. But some of the prisoners are better off from a health viewpoint than they were on the outside. We get a lot of them from Chicago who lived in slums all their lives and now at least they've got indoor plumbing and three squares a day."

Returning to the subject of Leopold, Ragen pulled several records from his desk drawer.

"Nate's I.Q. is supposed to be somewhere between 160 and 180," he said, "but he's never been given a suitable type I.Q. test. We've given him the Army Alpha test several times and he's always scored perfect. He seems to enjoy taking them—probably because it's a break in the routine."

As I was leaving his office, Ragen said he would have one of the guards take me on a tour of the penitentiary after my interview, provided I understood that guards are instructed to shoot to kill if visitors are ever taken hostage. I told him I would think it over and let him know.

A guard led me into a waiting room where I joined a number of other visitors passing the time of day. Every now and then a voice over an intercom system summoned one of us to the visiting room. When my turn came, I was beginning to get a bit nervous, particularly when I entered the room to find a guard seated on a small raised platform overlooking two rows of chairs facing each other. Between the two rows ran a long table which bore a line of division down the center and a partition of glass.

"Don't try to touch the prisoner in any way," the guard ordered me sharply. "Keep your purse on the floor and please obey any instruction immediately without question."

Leopold was escorted into the room from the other side and seated opposite me. Warden Ragen was right about his unprepossessing appearance, but at the age of forty-nine, Leopold was neither stooped nor broken as sometimes described in news stories. He was not tall—five feet, six and three-quarter inches—and he showed an inclination toward plumpness. But his bearing was erect, his eyes keen and his olive complexion free from any trace of prison pallor. He wore the regulation dark blue trousers, black shoes and blue pinstripe shirt open at the neck, and his dark hair was combed back smoothly from its faintly receding hairline.

My first impression of him was that he was constantly

watchful, as if not quite sure about my motive in interviewing him. His answers came slowly and carefully, particularly when relating to the subject of his parole hearing.

"I have no plans," he said, which I didn't believe. "The matter is in the hands of the parole board members and, no matter what happens, I intend to go on working, living up to life to the best of my ability and praying."

I felt that he was practicing a part of his planned speech before the parole board just to get my reaction.

"Let's talk about what you've done since you came in here," I suggested.

"Yes, let's," he said agreeably.

He spoke easily and without apparent strain as he traced his prison career through twenty-eight years. He had started his term performing factory work at what is now referred to as the "old branch" of the prison. After a few months there, he said, he was stricken with appendicitis at three o'clock one morning and rushed to the new Stateville branch for treatment. After his recovery, he remained—inmate No. 9306-D—serving his time quietly.

On the subject of his interests, he was eloquent.

"Medicine's at the top of the list, of course," he said, "and I like mathematics and languages."

"How many languages do you know?"

"Twenty-six."

"What's the latest you've learned?"

"Sanskrit."

"That's quite a list," I commented.

He looked at me suspiciously.

"Well," he said, "we have quite a bit of time in here, you know."

Nine years after starting his term, he told me, he cooked up the idea of getting a school started. He had put in seven years in the prison library where he installed a modern filing and checking system after most of the books were destroyed by a fire and new sets were made available.

"We really worked up the school from scratch," he said. "I wish you'd write a lot in your article about that. Studying in here. is a big factor in mental health. It's certainly much

135

better for a fellow to worry about a calculus problem rather than who's out with his wife while he's doing time."

When he began his project, he said, the only educational facility at the penitentiary was a "rather beat-up grade school for—well, practically illiterates."

After obtaining permission from the warden to inaugurate correspondence courses, Leopold and several fellow inmates launched the school. Prisoners were able to sign up for the courses, doing their homework in their cells in the evening hours and sending the results to the prison school for checking. Oral instruction in the school was limited to language courses and individual cases requiring special help.

"We've done pretty well," he told me. "We handle courses now from the eighth grade up, supplementing the prison grade school. I teach three times a week. I have two morning classes and one afternoon class—at 8:30 and at 9:30 in the morning and from noon to two in the afternoon."

He was quite proud of the school.

"You take Dr. William Johnson—do you by any chance know him? He's superintendent of education in Chicago. He's been here to see our school and has praised it highly. Once they even used our exams to administer to high school students in Chicago and the only complaint was from the students—that the exams were too stiff!"

He said that some of the inmates went on to college outside on the basis of their secondary preparation at Stateville.

"One of our boys was paroled at the time of the North African invasion," he said. "On the basis of the French he learned here, he was chosen liaison officer between our forces and the Free French of North Africa. Not bad. And we had another fellow who had trouble even reading a newspaper in his cell in Chicago. When he got here, he worked hard and wound up becoming a competent secretary. He was exceptionally good at Latin. He's out now."

I asked him if he had known another prisoner named Joe Macjek who was released after the *Chicago Times* had proved he was innocent of the crime for which he was convicted. Movie star Jimmy Stewart had played the role of the crusading reporter in the film based on Macjek's life titled "Call Northside 7777."

"Oh, yes," Leopold said. "He was another one who came here with a grade school education and when he left, he had two years of college. He worked very hard and deserved the break he got."

Leopold explained to me that when a man first entered the prison, he was required to take courses equivalent to the eighth grade if he needed them. At that point, if he wanted to continue his formal education, he could enroll in the correspondence school.

"My regular job is that of X-ray technician in the laboratory in the prison hospital," he said. "I worked for three years on the malaria tests in the parasitology and hematology laboratory of the hospital here. I've also done clerical and statistical work. And, oh yes, I donate blood regularly."

I must have exhibited surprise in my face—actually, I had thought a former malaria patient couldn't donate, but Leopold misinterpreted my look.

"Well," he said dryly, "even though I'm in here, I still have blood, you know."

I apologized and explained.

"I've had no malaria recurrence since 1945," he said. "I think those malaria tests were a very fine thing. A great many men who volunteered were honestly motivated and idealistic about it. I think they saw their chance to do their bit and embraced the opportunity. The tests started in 1944 and, by the way, we are still working on them. Some of the drugs developed are being used now in Korea—drugs such as primaquine, which is less toxic than pentaquine."

Here, he noticed my frantic effort to keep up with his conversation in shorthand.

"Would it help if I used the number of the drug instead of the name?" he asked politely. "It's SN 13272."

"What else have you done?" I asked him.

"Well, I've taken part in all the customary drives you people take part in outside. I also volunteered for the eye bank."

"How about giving me an idea of your typical routine in here?"

"I don't see anything interesting in that, but all right. I get up at 6:30 a.m.—is that the stuff you want? I sleep in the hospital, you see. I have breakfast, then go to work in the X-ray room at about 7:15. I have my lunch at 10:30."

"An odd hour for lunch," I commented.

He shrugged.

"Well, for some reason they set those hours that way here. Anyhow, that's nothing. I have my supper at 3:45. In the afternoon I spend an hour in the yard exercising. Then back to the lab where I work until about 11:00 p.m. On Saturday they have a baseball game here in the summer and a movie in the winter. I work on Sundays, too. Used to play handball a lot but I gave it up five years ago on the doctor's orders. Now I just take routine exercise."

How about visitors? He looked at me warily.

"We're permitted one visitor for fifty minutes every two weeks and we're permitted to write one letter a week. Incidentally, your visit is termed business and doesn't count as my regular visit. If it had, I'm afraid I might have been forced to decline to meet you."

"Are you in charge of the laboratory?"

"A convict isn't in charge of anything."

I set my pencil down on the table.

"All right," I said, "that's all for publication. Now, may I ask you something off the record and just because I'm curious?"

"Go ahead."

"What do you think of Adlai Stevenson from what you've read and heard about him?"

"Do you know him well?" he asked me.

"Pretty well, and I like him very much."

Leopold nodded.

"Yes—well, he won't be ruling on my case now. I understand that. So it doesn't really matter. But I watched his balcony speech on television. When I heard him, I was tremendously impressed. I thought about the Gettysburg Address—I really did. He must be a rare individual."

"Yes, he is," I said. "I just wondered what you thought of him."

I started to gather up my notes.

"Whatever happens," Leopold went on, "I'll always be grateful to the man for his courage in commuting my sentence. There are always people who will do what they think is right."

"He's one of them," I agreed.

"Yes, so is Dr. Einstein. He's another who went out of his way to help me."

"Einstein?" I asked, surprised. "Albert Einstein?"

"Yes, didn't I mention him? Perhaps not. When I first became interested in pursuing my studies in mathematics, I had a friend on the outside write him to see if he would be kind enough to suggest a curriculum. He did, and it was a tremendous help to me."

He gave me the name of his friend, we said good-bye and I wished him luck in his parole board hearing. But as I watched him turn away, I knew his chances weren't good at all.

Upon my return to Springfield, I wrote Leopold's friend, Dr. Ernest B. Zeisler, who lived on Lake Shore Drive in Chicago. He replied:

September 18, 1952

Dear Miss Milligan:

I have not seen Mr. Leopold for many years now and therefore can have no opinion of the purpose and the grounds for parole. I knew him when he was a young boy. I knew his two older brothers much better. I went to Stateville several times with his oldest brother at the suggestion of the latter, to discuss with the boy his interest in mathematics and in the Einstein theory in particular.

At that time, he wanted to study some books on the Einstein theory, and knowing that I had some familiarity with it, he had expressed to his brother the desire to see me. He wanted to write to Prof. Einstein and asked me to see that the letter got into his hands, and this I did. Prof. Einstein, with his constitutional kindness and warmth, took time to answer the letter, which letter I assume you saw at Joliet. Further I really have no comments.

Sincerely yours,
(signed) Ernest B. Zeisler

I had written Einstein at his home in Princeton, New Jersey, and received the following letter (complete with strike-overs in typing and signed in a tiny, cramped scrawl):

August 24, 1952

Dear Miss Milligan:

I remember that I have written to Mr. Leopold after having received a letter in his behalf from my friend, Dr. Ernest B. Zeisler (179 E. Lake Shore Dr., Chicago, Ill.). The correspondence is not in my files anymore; I recall, however, that I encouraged Mr. Leopold to study mathematics from books.

As I have no knowledge of Mr. Leopold's character and psychological situation I cannot form an opinion how his case should best be handled. In my opinion, such decisions should be made under exclusion of the resentment motive. The decision should depend on the answer to the question: Is it advisable from the standpoint of the interest of the community to give him the amount of freedom permitted within the limits of the law?

Sincerely yours,
(signed) A. Einstein
(typed) Albert Einstein

A few weeks later, after culling over my notes and reflecting on the matter, I decided that publication of the interview might revive criticism of Stevenson and even hurt Leopold's chances, dim though they were. I didn't need another by-line that badly.

As I had anticipated, Leopold was denied parole at the hearing early in 1953 under Stevenson's successor, Gov.

Nathan Leopold leaves the Illinois State Penitentiary following his parole. Photo courtesy Chicago Sun-Times.

William G. Stratton. Three years later, he lost out again, but in July of 1957 he made another try and this time was successful. He was released from Stateville Penitentiary on March 13, 1958, and immediately left for the Castaner Hospital in Puerto Rico to work as a technician. From time to time, I stumbled across an interview with him about his new life outside, particularly after he married in 1961. I also read his book *Life Plus 99 Years*, the royalties from which supplemented his hospital technician's salary of $10 a month.

Leopold earned his master's degree from the University of Puerto Rico and worked as a social service investigator with the Puerto Rico Department of Health.

In 1965, a news reporter wrote a feature story outlining Leopold's work on a three-year study project concerning the social factors in parasitic infection, one of the island's major health problems. At the World Health Organization's headquarters in Geneva, he had heard of a drug called fire orange A14 which appeared to have possibilities as a tracer material and was considered a breakthrough in the problem of parasite transmission.

In 1971, Leopold entered Mimya Hospital, Santurce, Puerto Rico, with congestive heart trouble. His personal physician, Dr. Ramon Suarez, Jr., said he remained at Leopold's side until shortly before Leopold's death. He said Leopold had insisted on the need to take the necessary steps to insure that his eyes would reach the medical institution promptly to be used in the eye bank.

Stevenson's farewell news conference in his mansion office after his 1952 defeat. Newsmen (left to right) are Tom Nelson, United Press; Jim Galloway, International News Service; Roy Harris, St. Louis Post-Dispatch; V. Y. Dallman (behind Harris), Illinois State Register; Charles Whalen (on Stevenson's left), Associated Press; Jim Klockenkemper, United Press; Jack Banton, reporter for Lindsay-

CHAPTER TEN

Interlude

There was never any thought in my mind that Stevenson's try for the presidency was to be his last. Although Eisenhower's plurality was about 6.5 million votes—33,936,252 to Stevenson's 27,314,992, Stevenson's percentage of the popular vote was 44.6 and this was about seven percentage points better than a private poll gave him at the beginning of his campaign.

Eisenhower took thirty-nine states in the Electoral College (a total of 442 votes) and Stevenson carried nine (89 votes). And all the states he carried were southern — Alabama, Arkansas, Georgia, Kentucky, Louisiana, Mississippi, North Carolina, South Carolina and West Virginia.

On the night before the election he told his followers:

"Looking back, win or lose, I have told you the truth as I see it. I am content. I have said what I meant and meant what I have said. I have not done as well as I should like to have done, but I have done my best, frankly and forthrightly; no man can do more, and you are entitled to no less."

For a man who was unknown to the general public just a few months earlier, he had done mightily well in his battle with a Goliath who exuded amiability and implied a supreme self-confidence which attracted voters like a magnet. Stevenson's inability to hide the doubts that all men feel on occasion, his refusal to put on a mask of perfection in public, his reluctance to expound confidently in nonsensical cliches— all these traits of his personality combined to defeat him. The voter wanted a man who would stand up and tell him that he had all the answers—and act like it! Between elections, the voter didn't want to be bothered with the business

143

of government. Besides, nobody paid any attention to him, anyway, except during a campaign.

Then, too, the familiarity of Ike's name as against the unknown from Springfield was too much to overcome. Familiarity may breed contempt elsewhere but in the arena of politics, it breeds success.

With the advent of Eisenhower's administration, Stevenson assumed the post of titular head of the party (he was quoted somewhere as saying "about as titular as you can get.") And into his job in Springfield stepped Republican William G. Stratton, who would proceed to undo much of the good accomplished there in the preceding four years. Here again was demonstrated the ambivalence of the voters. After enthusiastically sweeping Adlai into office as governor several years earlier, they just as enthusiastically turned around and swept in a man who was the opposite of everything for which Adlai stood! It was almost as bitter a pill to Stevenson as his defeat for the presidency—perhaps in some respects even more so.

When he gave his farewell address on January 8, 1953, Stevenson talked about future goals for Illinois and his hopes for their realization in the years to come. As for his own future, he said:

"Government—local, state and federal—is not something separate and apart; if it is to be good it must share the attitudes and the competence of the best in our society as a whole. Both business and government are gainers when the best among us from private life will make sacrifices, if need be, to fill vital positions."

For the ensuing two and a half years, Stevenson obviously enjoyed himself immensely, traveling around the world, making speeches, mending political fences and preparing for his next try. During this time we kept in touch intermittently by letter.

I spent those years in advertising and public relations work in Tulsa, Oklahoma, while marking time. I had made up my mind that I wanted to work for Stevenson on his next campaign and was prepared to go to considerable sacrifice to do this, even though I had no reason to feel that his chances of winning would be appreciably greater.

Aside from one brief hospitalization for a minor ailment, Stevenson remained healthy and apparently happy. At that time he wrote me that the doctors told him he would be his old self again some day, but he had his doubts.

His attitude toward politics seemed to me to be reflecting somebody's advice to get practical about it. After a long vacation in Barbados, he went to a Jefferson-Jackson Day dinner sponsored by Democrats in eleven Eastern states to deliver a "give 'em hell" type of speech. He took out after Secretary of Defense Charles Wilson's statement that "what is good for General Motors is good for the country" and suggested that the successor of the New Deal would be the "Big Deal." There was no scholarly vein to this approach and his partisan audience loved it.

The Democratic party must reaffirm its faith in all the people, he said, and in discussing the president and the Republicans, he offered this little gem:

"Our prayers go with them in the dark, the evil-haunted night we all must traverse, confronting an enemy whose massive power is matched only by its malevolent purpose."

It was sheer silly rhetoric, of course. Stevenson lunched with Eisenhower shortly after and found himself greeted warmly by a number of Republicans at the Capitol.

During his first six months as a private citizen again, Stevenson traveled extensively through thirty countries from Britain to Japan. He was accompanied by a *Look* magazine editor who later produced a big story and photo layout which didn't hurt Stevenson any.

In London, he was interviewed by the British Broadcasting Company about his plans regarding another run for the presidency and gave a typically Stevensonian answer:

"I am obliged to say to you that if I could answer your question—which I can't—I wouldn't!"

He received favorable — almost glowing — publicity elsewhere in magazines and in newspapers throughout the country. *Time* magazine sent a reporter to interview him at Libertyville after his global tour and wrote:

". . . the man who failed to win the last Presidential election but handsomely succeeded in winning respect and admiration everywhere is sorting out his impressions of America and the world and turning over and over in his mind the question of what, precisely, a man in his unique and not altogether enviable position ought to do."

He was deluged with letters of admiration and with invitations to speak and with suggestions that he write a book and with many many pleas that he run for the presidency again. He had about two and one-half years to pave the way before making an official announcement, and it was obvious to me from his activities that this was what he was doing.

His speeches and public statements during that period, while sometimes bowing to the exigencies of "practical politics," represented no departure in basic philosophy from his Springfield days. He would criticize the Eisenhower administration but not unjustly so in his own eyes. He would not try to destroy or castigate for publicity's sake. He hammered away constantly at the importance of nonpartisan statesmanship in areas of international concern.

In Chicago at a Democratic fund raising dinner on September 14, he stated:

"The structure of alliance is at issue. Moscow is using more seductive tactics. The world is weary, and we're on the threshold of momentous negotiations in Asia and Europe, Korea, China, Indochina, Germany. . . . The administration, and it is our government as well as the Republicans', must make fateful decisions that affect us all. The job of the Democrats is to help in every way we can."

On another occasion when he was making a report to the nation on his world trip, he described the poverty in Asia and prophesied that the rest of the world would be forced to pay more attention to India "and I suspect that as Europe's Eastern empires shrink, there will be left to us more of the burden of defense and of helping to guide the great forces which great changes have unleashed in Asia."

He went on to urge that negotiations be carried on with Russia—Stevenson often said that when negotiations ceased, war began. In his talk he said:

"At this moment a new fact confers a grim and pressing urgency on the international situation—the hydrogen bomb. For some years, efforts toward the limitation and control of armaments have been stalemated.

"Once more, I think, we should fix our sights high as we did in 1947, and resume the initiative in re-exploring the possibility of disarmament. The alternative to safety through an effective plan of arms limitation is safety through more massive spending and more frightening weapons development. . . .

"The quest for peace and tranquility isn't a day's work; it is everlasting. We will have to learn to think of the responsibility of leadership not as a passing annoyance but as a status in an independent world that we Americans, Democrats and Republicans alike, must live in, trade in, work in, pray for and pray for in the accents of mercy, justice and faith in a power greater than ours or any man's."

In the early part of 1954, Stevenson resumed his private law practice in Chicago with partners Bill Blair, Willard Wirtz and Newton Minow. But by the end of that year he would have made a total of at least eighty speeches, most of which were aimed at helping to elect Democrats running for gubernatorial and Congressional seats. Of course, he was not being altogether altruistic. I think he felt he owed it to the party to help out, certainly, but he was aware that this could aid his own campaign in 1955-56.

Republicans held 221 seats in the House of Representatives against 213 for Democrats. In the Senate there were forty-eight Republicans and forty-seven Democrats (with one independent). It was a situation in which a very few votes could decide the balance of power.

When the election was over in November, Democrats captured both the Senate and the House in addition to electing nine governors. Stevenson, obviously pleased at the result of his efforts, released the following statement:

"I have done what I could for the Democratic party in the past two years and now I shall have to be less active and give more attention to my own affairs."

News accounts during this period did not bear this out. He continued to give speeches—particularly concerning foreign policy and the situation involving the offshore islands of Quemoy and Matsu in China. He sounded very much like a man who was poised for another leap into the presidential campaign waters.

He was taking off the gloves more and more, hitting harder now and then at the administration and obviously becoming increasingly intent on voicing his disapproval of many of Eisenhower's actions. In defending Harry Truman from an attack by Atty. Gen. Herbert Brownell, Jr., Stevenson uttered these words:

"The Bill of Rights is besieged, ancient liberties infringed, reckless words uttered, vigilante groups are formed, suspicion, mistrust and fear stalk the land, and political partisanship raises strange and ugly heads, the security of secret files is violated, and the specter of a political police emerges."

He attacked McCarthyism and he went into a great deal of impassioned detail about the mortal struggle with world communism. On this latter subject he delivered a series of Godkin Lectures at Harvard University, which helped him not one bit in the political world and probably won him not one single follower because of the event's limited appeal— and that only to his host of followers who were being referred to now as "Stevensonites."

I was taken with an excerpt from another speech he gave during this period in which he said:

"And now in our time in spite of our devotion to the ideas of religious and secular humanism, I wonder if we are in danger of falling into a spirit of materialism in which the aim of life is a never-ending increase of material comfort, and the result a moral and religious vacuum. Is this leading, as lack of faith always must, to a deep sense of insecurity and a deterioration of reason? And I wonder, too, if today mass manipulation is not a greater danger than economic exploitation; if we are not in greater danger of becoming robots than slaves."

Back in Tulsa, I read a news item stating that Stevenson appeared to be gathering together a small, select staff of helpers who were beginning to look suspiciously like campaign staffers.

Putting through a telephone call to his Chicago office, I reached Bill Blair who told me Stevenson was out of the city and, after a brief explanation and a discussion of salary and arrival date, I found myself committed. It was that simple.

I was elated. Fortunately, I had no idea then what the inside of a presidential campaign would look like from a worm's eye view—particularly when I was the worm.

CHAPTER ELEVEN

The Unmaking of a President

Chicago hadn't changed any since I last saw it as a reporter. It was still big, loud, dirty and, when I arrived, coiled to lash us with one of its typically vicious winters. When I signed in, the month was November and the main topic of conversation was not what effect President Eisenhower's heart attack in Colorado would have on the presidential race, but whether or not Princess Margaret would marry Peter Townsend.

It was a fairly peaceful year—1955—which bode no good for Democrats who always seem to need a disaster of sorts in order to campaign to effect. Airlines were offering turbo-prop travel, railroads retaliated by advising "Be Safe and Sure—Travel by Pullman," and Chrysler was touting its new pushbutton powerflite transmission. On television, "I Love Lucy" was in its fifth year, Edward R. Murrow interviewed Julie Harris and John Gunther on "Person to Person," and one TV reviewer predicted that "George Gobel may have a rival in Johnny Carson, a minor-keyed CBS comic."

Vice President Richard Nixon addressed the New York Investment Bankers on CBS radio. Tammany boss Carmine De Sapio went to California to pick up support for Averell Harriman as a Democratic contender for the presidential race, and six top party leaders headed by California Atty. Gen. Pat Brown started a "draft Stevenson" movement.

"We're off and running!" Brown announced. "We want this movement to begin in the West and there's no turning back. We're in this until Stevenson releases us at the convention."

Back in New York, De Sapio retorted that such action was "panicky and hasty."

And in the midst of all this, nobody in Adlai Stevenson's headquarters in Chicago said anything. When I arrived at his offices in the Continental Illinois National Bank and Trust Company, I found that the candidate (whose official announcement had yet to be made) was out gallivanting around somewhere in the company of his chief aides (whoever they were) and that the remainder of his campaign staff consisted of a bevy of young women who were having the time of their lives enjoying the fringe benefits of life in Chicago.

Stevenson had leased slightly more than eight hundred square feet of office space on the eighth floor of the bank building at 231 South LaSalle Street in the Loop. Our campaign headquarters was about sixty yards from Stevenson's law offices, an austere, rather gloomy, wood-paneled suite which he shared with his three partners. The only other occupants were their secretaries, a receptionist (who ordered me icily out of her working area), and several clerical employees.

I learned early to stay away from that end of the hall as much as possible. Those people were the true "Stevensonites"—the loyal, dedicated, permanent staffers as compared with us opportunistic, transient hangers-on. They were the ones whose ties with Stevenson had been braided through years of personal service into a tough rope of possessiveness.

Two of the women in this suite of offices were particularly "devoted" to him. One of them had been with Stevenson for quite some time while the other was a comparative newcomer, and they were openly jockeying for his attention. The power struggle going on between them overawed me from the start.

I really didn't see what Stevenson could see in either of them, but the "old timer" of the two told me frankly that she was worried about her rival because "if you'll look closely at her, you'll see that she sort of looks like Ellen Stevenson, and you know how men are attracted to the same type."

Following her instructions, I found myself watching out of the corner of my eye and decided finally that there *was* a

152

slight resemblance. Also, it seems that Stevenson had invited the woman to dinner at his home in Libertyville one evening, which he shouldn't have done because the first woman took exception to this, called his housekeeper and astounded me by pumping her to "see if anything happened."

Apparently, all they did was eat. But Stevenson couldn't win. He unwittingly stirred her up again when he returned from one of his inevitable trips bringing back gifts for various staffers, and she found that her token of affection consisted of a bolt of cloth.

"He said I could make something out of it," she said in disgust. "God knows what!" — Which wouldn't have been quite so bad except that he brought the other woman a pretty piece of jewelry! One thing was certain—for all his charm, Stevenson was no lady killer.

Matters were more informal and less inhibited in the campaign offices down the hall where fourteen staffers, including myself, had been assembled from various sections of the country to form what was simply called "Stevenson Headquarters." In charge of Room 845 was Harry S. Ashmore, who was on leave from his job as executive editor of The Arkansas Gazette in Little Rock.

Harry, who was thirty-nine years old, was one of those "good old boys" loaded with charm, who got along equally well with both sexes and who, in an engaging "shucks, it wasn't anything" manner, would pass off his past accomplishments as just plain luck. To hear him tell it, he just happened to be in the neighborhood back in 1941 when they were giving away Neiman fellowships in journalism to Harvard. He had started his career in 1937, which wasn't the best year for anybody looking for a job, as a reporter columnist for the Greenville Piedmont in South Carolina.

Two years later, he was lucky enough to be hanging around when they needed a political writer on the Greenville News. From there he went to the Charlotte News in North Carolina where, when they needed an associate editor, there he was. A couple of years later, he stumbled into the job of editor and right after that he was offered the editorship of the editorial page of the Arkansas Gazette in Little Rock. A year later, he was made executive editor, which was his job when he took leave to join Stevenson.

Harry had written a book (with considerable research help from a team of educators) called *The Negro and the Schools,* and as he told it to me, "I was just lucky on my timing." The book created a sensation in the midst of the brewing desegregation battles of the early fifties and Harry found himself hired as a sort of expert on race relations for Adlai Stevenson.

(Harry's "luck" was to continue after leaving Stevenson's campaign in the spring of 1956. He returned to Little Rock where, two years later, he won a Pulitzer Prize for editorial writing in the wake of the rioting which followed the integration of a high school in that city. Harry also won the Sidney Hillman award and the Freedom House award and then went on to become a director for the Ford Foundation in Santa Barbara, California.)

He had been a combat infantry officer in the Ninety-fifth Division assigned to the Third Army in World War II, he told me, as we drank our lunch my first day on the job. He said he considered this his most valuable experience insofar as being prepared to hold his own on the campaign was concerned.

After finding out everything he could about me, Harry apparently decided that I wasn't too important, although it was obvious later that some of the other campaign staffers were darkly suspicious of my former ties with Stevenson. Harry was either more sure of himself or else he put on a good show of it. At any rate, he was possessed of the droll type of wit which I enjoyed and I found him good company to be around.

When we finished our lunch, he got up breezily, pulled my chair out for me and I promptly fell over the table. Thereafter, during the campaign I never again tried to match him drink for drink.

There had been some attempt to help campaign staffers in housing arrangements, but mostly for the men. The girls were doubled and tripled up in brownstone flats on the near North Side or, more or less, left to shift for themselves, while the men were located in the better Loop hotels. The housing arrangements made for me were worse than nothing. I was "bunked in" with a staffer who was a Chicagoan and had a two-bedroom apartment way out in South Chicago in the heart of "mugger land," and the only other staffer within hailing distance was Ashmore, who was occupying (with his wife and small daughter) a house just around the corner.

Commuting to and from the Loop was done via Illinois Central and also involved about eight long blocks of walking each day, as I was on straight salary and was given no expense account for taxi fare or unexpected costs. Had the other staffers shared the same grind, I wouldn't have complained, but the double standard prevailed throughout Stevenson's staff.

On November 11, Stevenson was busy making a speech in Charlottesville, Virginia, suggesting that guards representing the United Nations patrol the borders between Israel and Egypt. On the same day, Eisenhower flew back to Washington, and speculation increased that he would recover completely and run for reelection.

Two days later, a *New York Times* newsman named Richard J. H. Johnston described us campaigners in print as a bunch of "pros." In a rather lengthy story headed "STEVENSON READY WITH 1956 OFFICE," Johnston identified us by name and said that we had a "carefully fashioned political headquarters." I never had much faith in the *New York Times* after reading that.

Among other things, Johnston said that a Miss Ellen Bond, who was a former editorial assistant with *Harper's* magazine and a graduate of Barnard College in New York, had three assistants to help in the handling of the mail. Our headquarters, he said, handled an average of fifty letters daily addressed to Stevenson on political matters, and he quoted Miss Bond as saying that Stevenson read each of the letters and sent them back to her with marginal comments to be included in the answers.

This sent Ellen into hysterical laughter. Someone in the office had just sent a *form letter reply,* along with a note

suggesting that campaign contributions were always welcome—to a man named Gen. George C. Marshall!

Our press office consisted of a large room with two bat-
tered desks, two chairs, two typewriters and two telephones,
located next to Harry Ashmore's office, which also had a
desk, a chair, a typewriter and a telephone. Another room in
the headquarters "suite" was the big bullpen-workshop
housing the letter-answering team, a mimeograph machine,
a signature copying contraption and an automatic typewriter
which reproduced letters to make them appear personally
typed. Our so-called research office was headed by a young
man named John Brademas, who was from Indiana and who
went around looking intellectual. John was twenty-eight,
self-confident and, in his own opinion, brilliant. He had
been graduated magna cum laude from Harvard and had
been a Rhodes Scholar at Oxford. Before coming to Stevenson's campaign as an executive assistant, he had worked
briefly as a legislative assistant for U.S. Sen. Patrick Mc-
Namara and as administrative assistant to U.S. Rep. Thomas
Ashley. I never understood what he was talking about or
what he did and, after the campaign, he went on to Congress.

If I detected early an aura of provincialism in our headquarters, this seemed understandable to me when I got a
look at the first official list of staffers which included their
addresses. Of fourteen persons, I was the only one from the
Southwest. Ashmore, of course, was from Arkansas—then
we jumped to Wisconsin (Pigeon Falls), Indiana, Ohio, Pennsylvania, Connecticut, Massachusetts and New York.

I felt very much like a stranger until Stevenson returned
to Chicago, bringing with him the Chicago newsmen who
had been assigned to cover him—my old friends from Springfield. They all seemed glad to see me and we spent a few
good lunch hours talking. But I was more than a bit startled
when I learned that Stevenson had called our office and had
expressed complete astonishment that I was on his staff. I
had assumed that he had authorized my hiring, but apparently Bill Blair had taken it upon himself to do so and nobody had bothered to tell Stevenson who, fortunately for
me, seemed to think it was a good idea.

For the first time, I met the man for whom I would be working in the press office—a bespectacled, newspaper publisher named Roger Tubby, who had a high forehead, a clipped Eastern accent and a perpetually harried look. We barely had time to introduce ourselves and shake hands before plunging into a quick period of frenetic activity preceding Stevenson's formal announcement of his candidacy, which was scheduled for November 15, to be followed by a three-day meeting of the Democratic National Committee and a huge political rally at the International Amphitheatre.

To facilitate matters during this period, we staffers were assigned rooms at the Conrad Hilton Hotel on Michigan Avenue which was to be the site of activity swirling around Stevenson and his main rival, the as yet unannounced Estes Kefauver. At this point, Kefauver's candidacy for the nomination was taken for granted, and it was felt that several critical decisions involving primary battles would face Stevenson. If Stevenson did not enter any of the primaries (and he didn't want to) and Kefauver did enter, the Tennessee senator could win a large group of delegates by forfeit and win the nomination. On the other hand, if Stevenson was beaten in primaries in central populous states, he would have an uphill fight to win the nomination, and a dark horse candidate could take it.

Stevenson's announcement on November 15 was nothing more than a television production. The locale was the Conrad Hilton's Boulevard Room where boards had been placed over a rink on which an ice show was presented nightly and where the decor was strictly show biz. The candidate had been at his farm in Libertyville all morning and when he walked into the room, the stage directors shouted "Roll 'em!!" If Stevenson winced inwardly at this, he gave no outward appearance of his feelings. Instead, he smiled, waved his arms high like a boxer entering the ring and then seated himself in a green chair behind a desk facing the throng of newsmen and women. I recognized Dick Daley in the crowd as well as Jack Arvey, who was now Democratic National Committeeman, and Steve Mitchell, former Democratic National Committeeman. Jim Finnegan was there, too — the short, wiry little fifty-year-old Pennsylvania Secretary of State, who was going to be Stevenson's preconvention campaign manager.

Those were the "pros"—the ones who were supposed to give Stevenson's campaign the "new look" and provide the professional polish which would overcome Eisenhower's tremendous advantage.

Despite all the fuss and buildup, it was anticlimactic. Stevenson issued his statement, which said in part:

"In the first place, I believe it important for the Democratic party to resume the executive direction of our national affairs.

"Second, I am assured that my candidacy would be welcomed by representative people in and out of my party throughout the country.

"Third, I believe any citizen should make whatever contribution he can to the search for a safer, saner world."

He then announced Finnegan's appointment and said that Archibald Alexander, Democratic National Committeeman from New Jersey, would head a nationwide citizens group to promote the Stevenson candidacy. After a flurry of questions, Stevenson said he would make a further announcement the following day about the primaries and about additional staff appointments.

When I showed up for work the next morning, Roger Tubby greeted me with a frosty stare.

"Any idea where this story came from?" he asked me coldly, showing me a copy of the *Chicago Tribune*.

In a by-line story, George Tagge had written an excellent analysis of Stevenson's predicament concerning the primaries and had outlined his most probable course of action— right on the button. Tagge's story happened to appear right after Roger and several other top level staffers had discussed the matter in the press office in front of me. In a way, I could understand Roger's suspicions, but I also felt he was being unfair—particularly when I denied any knowledge of the source of the story, and he made it plain that he didn't believe me.

In a flare of anger, I picked up the phone and called Tagge to explain what I was up against. He certainly was sympathetic.

"Tell Tubby it's none of his damn business where I got it," he said. Then, apparently on impulse, he added: "Okay, I got it from Jim Finnegan—so what does he think of that?"

When I told Tubby, he started, mumbled something and turned back to his desk. He never did apologize to me.

At the news conference that afternoon, Stevenson announced that he would enter the Minnesota preferential primary, which was set for March 20. This was his only firm decision to date regarding the primaries, he said, and "the others we will consider when we come to them."

He also announced officially his staff appointments—Hy Raskin, Executive Director of the Campaign Committee (former deputy chairman of the Democratic National Committee); Roger Tubby, Press Secretary; C. K. McClatchy, Assistant Press Secretary; and Harry S. Ashmore, who is "going to advise me on substance, issues and problems."

McClatchy was the son of the McClatchy owners of a chain of pro-Stevenson newspapers in California—a young man who had volunteered for the campaign. On his application I had seen a note scribbled by Stevenson to the effect that the McClatchy newspapers were very important to the cause and that Tubby should find a place for C.K. Thereafter, Tubby and C.K. were to make the campaign trips with Stevenson throughout the country (C.K. complaining privately on occasion that he was just a luggage handler for the press) while I remained in the press office in Chicago handling a good bit of the routine drudgery and being utilized in emergencies as a trouble shooter with the Chicago press. Behind the smiles and the handshakes and the "welcome-aboards" of the staffers lurked the iron determination to hang onto one's turf. There was far more hostility among staffers than any displayed where the Republicans were concerned. In fact, I couldn't help suspecting that at least a few of the staffers were playing both sides of the fence where the politicians were involved, although not openly, of course.

The biggest mystery to me was where and how a presidential candidate dug up people qualified to work full-time on his campaign. Years later, when I saw the names of these people pop up regularly in other political areas, I was not so mystified. Most of them didn't just fall into these jobs the way I did. They were intensely ambitious individuals who got into politics intentionally and early, who worked their political connections as conscientiously and devotedly as any young businessman struggling upward on the corporate ladder, and who harbored no idealistic beliefs (and sometimes no beliefs at all!) about the candidate. Idealism, emotional attachment, personal involvement beyond surface companionability were the mark of the amateur. These people were the pros. In some cases, not very competent pros and perhaps not even very intelligent, but pros in that they traveled on the basis of their "connections" and had an unerring cannibalistic instinct when the chips were down.

At the time, I was surprised to hear so little talk of Stevenson's philosophy and beliefs. Most of what filtered down to me centered on personalities. The closest that any of the staffers ever came to thoughtful discussion was when Roger Tubby mentioned once that perhaps Stevenson was unable to relate to the American public because he seemed aloof. Tubby had served briefly as press secretary for President Truman in 1952, and he compared Stevenson with Roosevelt, speculating that FDR's battle with polio had been the major turning point in developing empathy with the public.

From what I knew of Stevenson, I was inclined to doubt this. If anything, I felt that he had had too much personal tragedy—the fatal shooting of his cousin during his childhood years*, a broken marriage, the deep disappointment of his first political defeat. Sometimes I felt that the wall around him was compounded of personal unhappiness and dissatisfaction within himself, and that, while he was basically a very sociable individual, he was not particularly interested in sharing his deep personal emotions with anybody.

---

* An incident which occurred when he was handling a supposedly unloaded rifle during a social gathering of youngsters his age in his home. A cadet had been demonstrating military drill and young Adlai had picked up the rifle which then discharged accidentally.

Tubby, who was forty-four and had impeccable old school ties which would appeal to Stevenson (Choate, Yale and the London School of Economics), struck me as being a bit on the cool side himself. Aside from four years as reporter and then managing editor of the *Bennington Banner* in Vermont, his journalistic experience was limited to his current role of publisher of the *Adirondack Daily Enterprise* in Saranac Lake, New York. His political and governmental ties, however, were priceless.

During the preceding thirteen years, he had worked as an information specialist for the Board of Economic Warfare, director of information for the Foreign Economics Administration and assistant to the administrator, director of the information office of International Trade in the Department of Commerce, press officer in the Department of State and assistant press secretary in the White House. He told me he also had worked in Albany, New York, in a governmental capacity.

Tubby was one of the pros about whom I would read later from time to time in the news columns. In 1960 he was to be named news director for the Democratic National Committee, in 1961 Assistant Secretary for Public Affairs for the Department of State, and in 1962 Ambassador and U.S. Representative to the European office of the United Nations and other international agencies in Geneva, Switzerland. These years, of course, were when Democrats were in the saddle and the plums went to their brethren. And this was the name of the game on a presidential campaign—you didn't work for the candidate; you worked for yourself.

It wasn't just a matter of money, either. It was power. There was something terrifically heady about being in the top echelon of government. Bill Blair, for example, was another who would find the early sixties a time for favorable winds and tide. He knocked down two U.S. Ambassador-ships—one to Denmark and another to the Philippine Islands. Later, he became head of the Kennedy Center in New York City and drifted out of the world of politics and back into the world of the beautiful people.

On Thursday, November 17, the Democratic National Committee opened its three-day meeting at the Hilton, and we staffers packed our little overnight bags and moved into the rooms which had been assigned to us. I had no idea what was going to happen, which was a good thing or I would never have gone there in the first place.

Kefauver got things off to a good start on Friday with a charge that the Democratic National Committee, whose chairman was Paul Mulholland Butler, was helping Stevenson instead of remaining neutral. Simultaneously, Stevenson announced the official opening of his "second campaign office" in the four-room Madrid Suite on the fifteenth floor of the Hilton. It was a garishly decorated suite overlooking Michigan Avenue with an elaborate bar at one end of the living room and toreador swords hanging all over the place. Up and down the corridor outside were rooms assigned to the various Stevenson staffers. At the end of the hallway was a large reception room with three doors—one opening into the hallway, another into the area where the elevators were situated, and a third into a small bedroom which was to be occupied by my roommate and me. In short, I had about as much privacy as if they had assigned me to perch on the chandelier in the lobby.

In the middle of the reception room was a long bar, behind which stood a white jacketed bartender amid several cases of assorted liquor and mix. My assignment, as I understood it, was to help several other young women "greet" officials and channel them back into Stevenson's suite. By "greet" I took it to mean that we were to be gracious hostesses who would extend hospitality to the gentlemen who entered and sort of keep an eye on who was coming and going. Which sounded all well and good early in the afternoon when everyone was sober, but by nightfall some of the gentlemen callers began to misinterpret our greetings. All I remembered clearly later was that the California delegation was first to show up—I saw that they had their drinks, took them back to the Madrid Suite and then returned to the reception room to find two other delegations swarming in.

At first, three staffers helped out but they soon got caught up in the social activity—and it was getting more social by the minute, what with several hundred men on the loose among a dozen females — and wandered off giggling and squealing on the arms of their new-found escorts. Before long, the corridors were packed with people, everyone shouting and waving drinks and pushing one another aside. They were popping in and out of hotel rooms like rabbits. Instead of greeting our guests graciously, I found myself running around snatching fifths of Old Taylor from their greedy little hands and protesting that "you can't have the whole bottle!" What worried me more than anything was what Stevenson's reaction would be when he found out that people were walking off with his liquor. I found him in the middle of a raucous, shoving crowd in his suite trying his best to carry on a conversation with Eleanor Roosevelt and Eric Sevareid, and though I hated to break up what was undoubtedly a profound discussion, I knew that the last of the big time spenders would want to know what I had to tell him. He was clearly irritated about it.

"Well, close down the bar, Pat," he responded exasperatedly, "Just close it down!"

Unfortunately, back in the reception room, nobody paid the least bit of attention to me when I shouted, "The bar is closed!" except the bartender who yelled, "Thanks! Good night!" and picked up his towel and left. The only thing I could think of was to haul the remaining bottles, two by two, into my little adjoining room and lock the door on them. The room obviously had not been intended for twin beds and there was so little space that I piled the bottles in the center of the floor where I had to step over them to reach my bed. And reach my bed I did—on the perfectly reasonable grounds that I couldn't do anything constructive for Stevenson in that bedlam outside, that I had already saved some of his liquor for him, and that I was tired and wanted to be left alone. I put my hair up in curlers, took a bath and went to bed.

When the pounding on the door woke me up an hour later, I found my roommate on the threshold. She had forgotten her key. Moreover, she told me, as she listed slightly to one side, everybody was having a party in another room and they had all decided to drive over to Mister Kelly's, a popular nightspot on the near North Side and wouldn't I like to come? I wouldn't.

Locking the door after her, I crawled over Adlai's liquor supply again and into bed. The pounding on my door was louder the next time, and when I opened it, my visitor was a newsman who gave me a silly grin and pitched forward face down onto the carpet, just missing the bottles by an inch or two. There he lay—the top half of him in my room and the bottom half outside in the reception room, which was now dark and quiet. It took me quite some time of prodding and pushing and pulling to get him to his feet and convince him that he couldn't stay. Just as I propped him upright in my doorway, the light in the reception room snapped on and there stood Senator Sparkman of Alabama and three other men, who had come back for God knows what reason and who were as surprised as I was to see anybody there. There was no sense trying to explain anything to anybody. They saw what they saw—me and a reeling newsman in a hotel room with a couple dozen bottles of booze—and as I shoved the half-unconscious newsman all the way out and closed the door, all I could think was, "Oh, well, how likely am I to ever run into Senator Sparkman of Alabama again?"

I ran into him the following evening at the International Amphitheatre where the Democrats were holding a $100-a-plate dinner for some twenty-eight hundred loyal followers, but if the senator recognized me, he pretended he didn't. The main speakers of the evening were Stevenson, Kefauver and Averell Harriman, who was trying to look like the perfect "dark horse." Former President Truman spoke briefly, too—he made it clear that Harriman, not Stevenson, was his man this time—and people applauded, but not too wildly because we Stevensonites outnumbered them, and a number of drunks staggered around and it was all very uninspiring.

The first snow of the year had fallen and I had been forced to struggle with Chicago's public transportation system to get out to the Amphitheatre while the higher echelon campaign staffers went by private car. My paycheck wouldn't cover taxi fare. It was a long way to go for a free dinner and not worth it and I was glad when it was all over.

Just getting to and from anywhere in that city was a struggle of heroic proportion, particularly when the struggle took place through snow and sleet and ice and the early darkness of winter, which tempted muggers and rapists to slither out from under their rocks and go hunting for prey. The men on the campaign were singularly unconcerned about this until one of them went out into the night and got mugged. Thereafter, we were all advised to call a certain taxi company with whom arrangements had been made to haul us home after dark. Their drivers had been checked thoroughly, we were told, to make certain they were not rapists who were moonlighting.

Of course, no arrangements were made to pay the taxi fare for us, so I continued to go home the hard way — hiking through the Loop to the Illinois Central Station, standing in the crowded, smelly, swaying train all the way to the Hyde Park stop and then trudging another four blocks to my apartment. A couple of times I was able to catch a taxi ride with Harry Ashmore, whose apartment was right around the corner, and who was on an expense account. But usually, I just took my chances.

After the snows came and stayed, I clomped around in heavy boots and coat with a woolen scarf wrapped around my head and, since nobody mugged me, it was possible that I was mistaken for some old derelict not worth slugging. But, being wiser to Chicago's ways than the out-of-state campaigners, I never took the chances they took. Ashmore's wife shared my views. She told me that when she and Harry moved into their apartment, the first thing they saw was that the windows had bars.

"We didn't have bars on our windows back in Little Rock," she said grimly to me. "If they've got bars here, there's a reason. They're to keep something out that wants to get in."

I didn't mention to her that just the other day, two men had taken a door right off the hinges in my apartment building in daylight and had ransacked the place.

As time went on, the "glamour" of working on the inside of a presidential race began to wear right down to gravel. In fact, whenever I looked around the headquarters office, I couldn't help thinking how basically disjointed the whole structure was—like a skeleton held together loosely with baling wire because somebody ran out of bones. It was somewhat startling to realize that we were going for the most powerful position in the world.

I doubt that my growing disillusionment was shared by the other staffers, however, as they seemed to enjoy the campaign without worrying about what was happening to the candidate. In fact, I envied their seeming ability to operate in the thick of things as if in the calm eye of the hurricane. Every time a celebrity showed up, they dropped everything and had a fine time acting as escort around the headquarters or just plain eavesdropping on what was going on.

One of the girls almost went into hysterics the day Harry Belafonte showed up, and she ran down the hall screaming:

"He's beautiful! He's just beautiful!"

(Apparently his beauty didn't sway Stevenson any as we heard later that Belafonte stormed out, angry because he felt the candidate wasn't taking a strong enough stand on civil rights.)

Another visitor was a well-known movie star who, according to Stevenson's secretary, was "just crazy about him" and kept calling him at his Libertyville home. Some of the staffers wound up in a Loop nightspot one night with her and her entourage of Hollywood friends, reporting later that she put through long distance calls to Frank Sinatra from their table in which they passed the phone around exchanging happy insults.

I passed up the occasional invitations to share in all this glamour for the very practical reason that I was afraid to be out alone after dark. From experience, I learned early in the campaign that I was living too far out of the Loop to expect any man to see me home safely. In fact, Chicago's taxi drivers frequently turned me down when I splurged and flagged them down. They didn't want to drive all the way out to the

South Side when they could make short trips from the Loop to the Near North nightspots and pick up more in tips.

Anyone who has never lived in Chicago cannot fully appreciate the assault upon the senses during the winter months — the sooty phlegm in the throat and nostrils, the steamy discomfort of sweating feet in heavy boots, the nerve-wracking dissonance of taxi horns, bus motors, police whistles all playing a shrill concerto.

Snowfall packed down upon snowfall. Bundled up like a Cossack, huddled over against the whipping wind from the river, I would clomp along feeling my toes go numb—little toes first, then the toes next to those, then on across my feet with my big toes the last to lose sensation.

Lunch hours were particularly unpleasant. Unable to afford the better places, I sat at counters gulping my food while people lined up behind me waiting for me to finish. This didn't seem to bother seasoned Chicagoans the way it did me. I admired the aplomb with which some of them not only polished off dessert at a slow pace but lit cigarettes and enjoyed a leisurely after-luncheon smoke oblivious to the people lined up right behind them. I couldn't do it. Usually, I either grabbed a fast pizza in a five-and-ten where I stood eating it in the aisle or I brought a cold meat sandwich with me to the office.

Understandably, I wasn't very sympathetic when Roger Tubby and C. K. McClatchy returned from campaign swings to Florida and California complaining, as they once did, about the quality of the steaks they had been served.

Shortly before Thanksgiving, Stevenson officiated at the opening of the "National Stevenson For President Committee Headquarters" in a building just a couple of blocks from our campaign headquarters. As one of the wire services was unable to send a reporter, the bureau chief asked me if I would cover for them. I decided to take shorthand notes on most of the interview and then transcribe them word for word without editing, just to see how Stevenson put his words together under fire. The result was interesting:

Question:	Governor Harriman said at his press conference yesterday that—many things which Stevenson said I would not have said, and he said many things which I would have said differently. What is your comment on that, sir?
Stevenson:	I only say nice things about him. Did he say something different? Otherwise, it would be plagiarism.
Question:	Can you go into the purpose of this headquarters, what it is called and why it is being set up?
Stevenson:	There have been a lot of phone calls and mail and correspondence for the past several weeks. In an effort to coordinate those offers of help, I have asked my old friends, Barry Bingham of Louisville and Mrs. Edison Dick if they would become co-chairmen of an organizational committee and if they would set up these central offices and give advice and counsel to local and regional organizations around the country. They agreed to do so and these rooms, which I hadn't visited before, are the result. This is called the Stevenson for President Committee instead of Volunteers for Stevenson, of which Mr. Bingham and Mrs. Dick are co-chairmen. They have also recruited the services of Archibald Alexander, another old friend of mine. I believe that this has been announced earlier.
Question:	Why the other name? Did the first one not turn out to be fortuitous?
Stevenson:	You'll have to ask them—I just don't know.

(Mrs. Dick intervened here)

Mrs. Dick:	This is a pre-convention operation, not a post-convention one. In order to differentiate it from the other one, it seemed to be the most descriptive, and it embraces everyone who wants to work.
Question:	How do you reconcile your speech Saturday night, Governor, in connection with moderation in view of Truman's stand for a liberal and progressive program?
Stevenson:	Well, I hope mine was a liberal and progressive program. I always thought I was liberal and

progressive so I don't know whether any reconciliation is necessary.

Question: Do you feel the country's in need of liberal moderation?

Stevenson: There is one battle I won't get into and that's the one of semantics. If you took the trouble to read my speech of last Saturday night, I said don't confuse mediocrity with moderation.

Question: How do you feel about the meetings of the Democrats last week?

Stevenson: I feel very fine. I feel very exhilarated and reassured by the state of mind of the Party which I thought was both healthy and realistic. I don't believe there was any false overconfidence and I also felt that there was a great eagerness and heart for the contest.

Question: How do you explain the fact that nineteen Democratic governors failed to show up?

Stevenson: I suppose they couldn't come. I never went to any while I was governor.

Question: What is the distinction between this Committee and the regular Campaign Committee?

Stevenson: This Committee is to coordinate all the offers of help and material which do not come to the regular Democratic organization.

Question: Kefauver's lease is paid up through next year. How is your lease paid up here?

Stevenson: I really don't know. I hope it is paid up at least through next week. You will have to ask them.

Newsmen: Thank you, Governor Stevenson.

On Thanksgiving Day, we out-of-state staffers were invited by Stevenson to his home in Libertyville—a thoughtful gesture on the part of a man embroiled in a presidential campaign. I had never seen him so exuberant—except back in Springfield after a legislative victory. Things seemed to be falling into place for him and he appeared to enjoy himself immensely showing us around his seventy-acre farm which, even in the leafless austerity of gray winter, was impressive with its two-hundred-yard driveway and its flock of black-faced Suffolk sheep and its maple trees. He told us that he kept the sheep for a pastoral effect so that his Republican neighbors would tend to consider him more a gentleman farmer than a crass politician.

His twelve-room house was a charming blend of tastefully assembled period pieces—a comfortable place with airy rooms and fireplaces and that old American longed-for atmosphere of gracious living which only money can get you. It was considerably less formal than the governor's mansion in Springfield, yet there was something about the day that seemed remarkably familiar, even though I had never been in his house before. As Stevenson bustled around in his worn brown jacket and loud red shirt and somewhat baggy slacks trying to make everyone feel at home, taking orders for our one drink before dinner and handing them out, I had the distinct feeling that I was reliving something.

When we sat down to dinner, it came to me suddenly. I was the only "old friend" in the room. Everybody else was a comparatively new face in his life and he was knocking himself out for them—not me. I was seated at his left at dinner, which made it convenient for him when he went into his act. No wonder it all seemed familiar! So many times in Springfield at news conferences and at mansion get-togethers he had done this.

"On the way out here, Governor," I told him, "somebody whipped out a copy of one of your speeches and read it to see what we thought of it. Now, really, on a holiday, I thought that was going too far! We're supposed to get away from it all, don't you think?"

"Of course!" he agreed with me. Then, pausing for effect, he asked in mock eagerness:

"But tell me, Patricia, what did you think of my speech?"

He fairly preened at the laughter of the other staffers.

After dinner, we drifted down to his recreation room in the basement. The place looked like a garage sale. He had hung souvenirs from his world travels all over, including African spears, a couple of shrunken heads, blowpipes, things that appeared to be old shawls, and all kinds of bric-a-brac which he apparently felt added to the decor—whatever that was. He seemed to have hauled half of Europe and Asia back with him the way some people bring home Kewpie dolls and purple pillows inscribed "Mother" from the county fair.

"How do you like it?" he asked me proudly.

In one corner was a small display which interested me— several newspaper clippings carefully preserved under glass. Stevenson watched as I glanced over stories by-lined John Dreiske and George Tagge and Charles Wheeler and Hub Logan—all from Springfield days.

"I didn't know you saved these," I exclaimed.

"Well," he said, "I really had about two or three times this number, but I culled them down. I thought these were the most interesting."

They seemed to be a good cross section of the highlights of Springfield, I noted — the unfavorable along with the favorable.

"You know, Governor," I said, as I surveyed them, "you'd be surprised to know how many friends you had among the press in Springfield."

Instantly, his pleasant smile vanished and he stared at me incredulously. Then, in an icy tone, he snapped:

"I certainly would!"

CHAPTER TWELVE

Finale

Back in the campaign offices after the holidays, matters weren't getting any better between Roger Tubby and me. It was one of those situations involving a tremendous amount of misunderstanding, lack of communication and a growing resentment on my part at being utilized more and more in menial office chores. I was so close to the Chicago political editors that I'm sure Roger was afraid to tell me anything for fear I would pass it along to them. Actually, it was the other way around.

One of the news magazine editors, a man I had not met before joining the campaign, tipped me off that Roger had decided to have me transferred to the "Volunteers for Stevenson" group which was just then moving into new offices a good many safe blocks away from the campaign headquarters. I was stunned. Roger had said nothing to me about it. Also, I didn't know whether or not to believe the editor who had tipped me.

A few days later, Stevenson's secretary excitedly called me to tell me that she had news for me.

"Good or bad?" I asked.

"I don't know," she replied. It seems the "Volunteers for Stevenson" had requested my services.

At that point, I really didn't care too much about staying on in the press office but I didn't like the idea of being shoved out, either. I decided to fight it out. When Roger returned from his latest campaign swing, I confronted him without any warning.

"You may have heard rumors," I said, "that I'm trying to transfer to the 'Volunteers for Stevenson' group. I know how that stuff gets around because I've heard the rumor myself.

I have no idea where it came from but I wanted you to know that I'm not a bit interested and there's no truth to it as far as I'm concerned."

He blinked at me, obviously startled, and replied rather vaguely that he was happy to have me stay on. Later, I wondered if I had gained anything by forcing the issue. My unhappy situation remained.

Shortly after that, the magazine editor told me that he had had lunch with Roger a couple of days after I had joined the campaign and that Roger had mentioned that he thought I would be happier with the "Volunteers." It was obvious to me that I was not staying in my place obediently handling the clerical work doled out to the female staffers and waiting on the men. I had not joined with aspirations of a top job. Those plums went to men, not women. This was 1955 and nobody cared if I considered myself treated unjustly—least of all, the men for whom I was working.

But I had not expected to be shunted into office work with no chance of helping out in press relations, an area in which I could have helped Stevenson greatly, particularly since his relations with the Chicago press were so poor. Even the Chicago newsmen commented on this. As peculiar as it sounds, Stevenson was happily giving speeches in Washington, D.C., where the residents (at that time) could not even vote and in New York, where his political strength was passably strong—and ignoring the weak spots.

As in Springfield, he seemed to have no idea how to deal most effectively with the press, and it seemed to me that he was taking the advice of people who had no idea, either.

In addition, Stevenson's inexperienced "advisers" just weren't playing in the same ball park when the *Chicago Tribune* went after him on what was known in the campaign as "the farm issue." He had been burned on this issue during his first campaign.

All good candidates for political office are required to go back to the old hometown for a visit, start attending church (even if this means hastily joining one), wear funny hats and graciously accept souvenirs and gifts. During Adlai's first campaign, he set out in his chauffeured limousine (followed by several press cars filled with newsmen and photographers) to visit his farm south of Bloomington—and couldn't find it! Up and down the good old country roads the chauffeur drove, stopping occasionally at a farmhouse to ask directions. All of which left the newsmen more or less convulsed with laughter.

This should have made him more cautious during his second campaign when it came to farm issues. Instead, he took the advice of his top aides to level off at U.S. Secretary of Agriculture Ezra Taft Benson on the grounds that the country's farmers were going broke.

The *Chicago Tribune's* enterprising Dick Orr drove out to the farm where he dug up from farmers in the area the information that Adlai was a "tightwad" and wouldn't spend any money on the place. It seems he had a professional farm manager—a boyhood chum of his who told Orr that he, personally, was a great admirer of Benson's and that Adlai's farm was a moneymaker even though it was located in a poor section of McLean County.

Dick capped off his story with an account of his phone call to Stevenson's brother-in-law, Ernest Ives, in which he asked:

"Is the farm making any money?"

To which Ives nonchalantly replied:

"Of course. All good Illinois farms are making money!"

The moral to this, as far as I was concerned, was that all relatives of political candidates should be told in advance to "shut up."

In early December, I was working late in the press office when the phone rang. The caller, a gentleman from the City News Bureau, informed me cheerfully that Adlai Stevenson had just crossed a picket line at the airport while on his way to New York City to address an AFL-CIO convention. My first reaction to this horrifying piece of news was that he probably *had!*

I knew that Stevenson had left for the airport just moments earlier to board a United Airlines flight for New York and it seemed perfectly plausible that he and his whole damned staff of experts could do something like that.

"Are you sure?" I asked the newsman.

"I got a picture of him," he snapped.

All I could do was tell him that Stevenson was on the plane (true) and that I would check out the story (true) and that I was sure there was some mistake (true—on Stevenson's part).

When I hung up, the phone bleated again—and again—and again—and again. After all, it wasn't every day that a presidential nominee crossed a picket line en route to a big labor convention!

I kept assuring them that I was checking it out and would get them a statement of fact as fast as I could. Between calls from the press, I found out that there was indeed a strike in progress by the Flight Engineers International Association, and that some mysterious individual had tipped off the City News Bureau that Stevenson and two other men had not honored the picket line. As Bill Blair and Roger Tubby had accompanied Stevenson, this additional information hinted at a chill of truth to the incident. Just as I had left word in New York for Tubby to call me upon arrival, I heard from the *New York Times* man, Richard Johnston.

"They crossed a picket line all right," he told me, "but you've got one alibi going for you. It's not much but better than nothing. It seems that it was just a one-man picket line and apparently they didn't see him."

At that moment, I heard Harry Ashmore in the next office drawling in an almost nonchalant tone into his phone:

"No—no truth to it, so far as we know. No truth at all."

Hastily, I rushed in and signaled him.

"He did, Harry!" I hissed. "He crossed a picket line!"

Harry, who had been talking to the *Chicago Sun-Times* man, dropped the receiver.

"Oh, damnation!" he blurted, stunned. "And on his way to a labor convention! Just what we need!"

For the next hour or so, we worked the story together, getting the name of the one-man picket, ascertaining that City News Bureau was bluffing and did not have a photo, and forcing the union official to admit that the picket might not have been seen by Stevenson. Midway in our work,

Roger Tubby called from New York with a not very helpful statement for me to release, which asserted that they had seen no pickets, were unaware of the strike and that "it is and has been Stevenson's policy to respect the union position in any legitimate labor dispute."

When it was all over, Harry and I shared a cab out to the South Side and as he opened the cab door for me, he was obviously still a bit shaken, but regaining his composure.

"This night," he said sardonically, "will be indelibly etched in my memory. I haven't had so much fun since World War II."

On December 16, Senator Kefauver announced his candidacy and his intention to enter "a number" of state primaries in conducting what he called "a vigorous campaign." Specifically, he named California as one primary he would enter, and he indicated strongly that he would file in New Hampshire's March 13 primary. By that time, Stevenson had announced he would enter primaries in Illinois, Florida, Pennsylvania and California, as well as Minnesota.

When Kefauver made his announcement, Stevenson was keenly interested in getting the full story immediately so that he could issue a statement, but we did not subscribe to a news service (which I considered an appalling oversight on somebody's part!) As I was the only staffer well enough acquainted with the Chicago press, I was asked to obtain the wire service copy, if possible. In return, I promised the wire service the first call on Stevenson's reaction to Kefauver's entry. Stevenson was delighted when I brought the copy in to him and obligingly gave me his handwritten statement scribbled on a piece of scratch paper:

Kefauver statement —

Senator Kefauver is an esteemed friend and I say come on in; the water's fine. I am glad to hear that he wants to increase the unity and strength of our party. Certainly we shall need unity and strength next November for this important contest.

Adlai E. Stevenson

Most of us out-of-state campaigners intended to go back to our homes for Christmas, and when Stevenson heard of this, he decided to have a party for us in advance. This time, we spent the first part of the evening at a so-called guest house on the William McCormick Blair estate before driving over to Libertyville. There we each had a couple of drinks and potato chips served from a silver tray by an unsmiling butler and wandered around admiring Bill's indoor tennis court and marveling at the strange ways of multi-millionaires.

Arriving at Adlai's home later, we milled around in the living room for a time looking at his Christmas decorations (he had a tree on which were hung little blue donkeys!) while awaiting our buffet dinner. The two drinks from Bill's place began to wear off. Finally, Jane Dick asked me if I would like a drink.

"Certainly," I said, "but I don't think we're going to get one."

"Follow me," she said confidently.

I was hesitant about traipsing into Stevenson's kitchen, but Jane was an old family friend of his and she knew where he kept his liquor supply. Back we came triumphantly bearing our drinks, which we set on a coffee table. She had no sooner downed hers and joined a group in a far corner when Stevenson approached, his steely gaze fixed upon my drink.

"Where did you get that, Pat?" he asked me.

I told him.

"Hmmmm," he said grudgingly. "Well, go ahead and finish it." He was quite disapproving.

What was supposed to be a lull in the campaign until after Christmas was shattered on December 21 when Stevenson's nineteen-year-old son, John Fell, was seriously injured in an automobile accident near Goshen, Indiana. The incident also underscored Stevenson's difficulties with his former wife, who had never recovered from her emotional turmoil after the divorce.

Young John was driving home from Harvard University for the Christmas holidays when an approaching truck driver swerved over a culvert attempting to pass another car, and the Stevenson car was hit head-on. All that saved John from death was the fact that he tried desperately to steer between the approaching car and the truck when he saw that a collision was inevitable. Two fellow students in his car were killed and John sustained severe knee injuries and lacerations.

When news of the accident reached us in the campaign office, Stevenson immediately flew from Meigs Field in a chartered plane with Bill Wirtz, Roger Tubby and Dr. James Stack, a Chicago bone specialist, returning the following day in an ambulance transporting John to Passavant Hospital for further treatment. The air of depression which had settled over us began to lift when we heard that John would recover, and everyone pitched in to help answer the telegrams and cards and notes of condolence which had started to pour in from all over the world.

Back in the office, Roger told us that the worst part of the whole incident, as far as he was concerned, came at Passavant when he had to maneuver Stevenson and the former Mrs. Stevenson in and out of the hospital so that they did not meet in full view of the press. The volatile Ellen was not noted for her taciturnity. His secretary told me once that she called him frequently at his office, demanding crisply to speak to "Mr. S." and keeping him on the line with complaints—mostly about publicity.

As a special Christmas present for us, Kefauver filed for the Minnesota primary, as well as the one in Wisconsin, but this didn't dampen our campaign managers because, as they kept saying, we were favored to walk away with Minnesota. It was obvious, however, that the preconvention battle was on and would be as grueling as the newsmen had been predicting.

Returning from my Christmas holiday trip, I found that our letter-answering people were still on the ball. I had received a form letter "thank you" in reply to my note of condolence to Stevenson about John Fell. I also found in a separate envelope a statement from Stevenson which was not addressed to anybody in particular but merely typed on his letterhead stationary, dated and signed "AES." It read:

179

Following are some ideas that I want to develop, if you agree:

This Republican administration is the first government we have had which has realized and taken advantage of the fact that today support and opinion can be manufactured for almost any person and any cause. No matter how much personality, power, energy, brains and character you possess, you cannot fight this political battle on the old-fashioned individualistic basis. I am afraid it takes more to counteract and that propaganda has to be combated with propaganda.

In our modern mass society we live exposed to the greatest flood of mass suggestion any people has ever experienced. Only a few know that Eisenhower's reputation and that of his associates is for the most part manufactured. But there is no use deploring either the results or the methods used. They have to be met by a well-organized counterattack and by whatever additional advantages the candidate may have. In a collective age don't we have to use more collective methods? This is probably a matter which relates more to the campaign than to the primary. What are we doing about it, or, rather, what is being done about it, with a view to the possible convention period?

Should I send this to Paul Butler, to Clayton Fritchey, et al, or is it all so obvious that no advisory and planning committee need be established? Or is there one?

AES

I don't know who answered this plaintive note—if anybody, but shortly after, I was appalled to receive what was intended to be an authoritative, official, professionally processed "Press List." This quaint little document, typed on yellow scratch paper, read in full:

PRESS
      P-1   — Chicago Press List
      P-2   — Miscellaneous Press List
      P-3   — Negro Press
      P-4   — Labor Press
      P-5   — Language Press
      P-6   — Farm Press

P-7 — Columnists & Editorial Writers
PMD — Minnesota dailies
PMW — Minnesota weeklies
RADIO-TV
    R-1 — Commentators (National except Washington)
    R-2 — Farm Directors (National)
    R-2M — Farm Directors (Minnesota)
    R-2F — Farm Directors (Florida)
    R-3 — News Editors etc. (National except Washington)
    R-3M etc.
GOVERNOR'S LISTS
    G-1 — Those who get everything
    G-2 — Those who get stuff & things
ORGANIZATIONAL
    0-1 — SPC's
    0-2 — Unofficial
    0-3 — Democratic organizations
    0-4 — Candidates

The code which interested me most was G-2 under GOV-
ERNOR'S LISTS—those who get *stuff* and things.

We were getting more and more professional in the field
of public relations, it seems. Somebody hired a public relations man from Washington, D.C., who went to work immediately and, in early March, produced a six-page memorandum on legal size paper describing campaign materials
available to us. Among other items listed were lapel tabs,
four-color bumper stickers, four-color window stickers,
large posters of Stevenson in black and white on a blue
background with the legend "Vote for STEVENSON," one-
column newspaper mats, photos, a new publication called
"The Stevenson Newsletter," a Stevenson leaflet which consisted of a two-color summary of his biography, accomplishments and opinions on important issues, a full set of twenty
20-second TV spots, four 30-second spots and two five-
minute spots for each of the primary contests in Minnesota,
Illinois, Florida, Pennsylvania and California, radio spots
and—as I could hardly wait to point out to Harry Ashmore—
also a twelve-page leaflet of key excerpts from Stevenson's
address to the AFL-CIO Convention in New York City!

The memorandum was dotted with impressive sounding instructions about billings, distribution, glossy prints, proofs, scheduling, open-ended spots, audio and discs. There were even suggestions to women on where to place the Stevenson tabs—on belts, collars, scarves, handbag straps, pockets, hats and everywhere except on their rear ends. It seems the tabs were selected instead of pins because they cost so much less, but it was admitted that ladies could not wear tabs on blouses or sweaters very easily.

With all this ammunition behind us, we swung into the Minnesota primary with gusto. At least, the "pros" did. I didn't know how Stevenson really felt, but I was approaching a decision to resign from the campaign, a decision not easily reached at that stage because I knew that Stevenson would interpret it as pessimism over his chances of winning. When I joined the campaign, I had not thought about the possibility of victory. I was under no delusions one way or the other. But I also knew that my departure from the campaign—particularly before the national convention, which was often the big lure in hiring staffers—would attract some attention, and I wanted to slip away as quietly as possible. I knew the news business well enough to realize that timing was the important thing and that, once I was miles away, the press wouldn't pursue the matter.

Actually, I had considered resigning at least once before Christmas on grounds that my experience in news and press relations was not being utilized, and I had had a long discussion with one of the Chicago political editors about this. He urged me to quit and even tipped off the *New York Times* man, Richard Johnston, that I might be interested in an offer. Johnston called me, but the salary he quoted on a job in the Chicago bureau was $80 a week!

"How could I live on that in Chicago?" I gasped.

"Well," he said, "a lot of our beginning staffers get help from their parents."

I wasn't that impressed with the *New York Times*. I was beginning to want to put a lot of distance between me and the Chicago scene. I felt that Stevenson had surrounded himself with people who were not even well-intentioned, let alone professional, and that he was like a swimmer trying to get along diplomatically with a school of piranhas. More and more, I felt that I couldn't help him.

On the evening of March 20, I joined several staffers at what was intended as a victory party in a brownstone apartment building on the near North Side where we had gathered to listen to the returns of the Minnesota primary and celebrate. Stevenson was at his Libertyville home with Mr. and Mrs. Bill Wirtz, Edison and Jane Dick, and George Ball. After it was all over, we sat around unbelieving in an atmosphere of black despair. Somebody came in and quoted Stevenson as saying privately: "Dammit, I'm tired of losing!" Kefauver had upset him, winning twenty-six of the thirty delegates and leading by a sixty thousand-vote margin of victory. Of course, Kefauver had been helped by the Republican crossover vote, but that still wasn't large enough to account for the upset.

The following day at his office, Stevenson issued a formal statement through our press office:

STATEMENT BY ADLAI E. STEVENSON

March 21, 1956

> Office of Roger Tubby
> Stevenson Campaign Committee
> 231 S. LaSalle Street
> Chicago, Illinois

While I was personally disappointed by the Minnesota results, I hope no one will miss the real point in yesterday's primary. It was a smashing repudiation of the present administration and a two to one endorsement of Democratic principles by the people of Minnesota.

I do not propose to conjecture about the possibility that thousands of loyal Republicans may have voted in the Democratic primary for the cynical purpose of damaging the Democratic Party in Minnesota or me.

I consider the results full notice that the great swing back to Democratic principles which started in 1954 is even stronger in 1956.

Senator Kefauver has won the first round and I congratulate him. As for myself, I will now work harder than ever, and I ask my kind friends everywhere to redouble their efforts, too.

As I said last night, my plans are not changed, and neither are my ideas. I have tried to tell the people the truth. I always will. I have not promised them the moon. And I never will. This may not be the way to win elections but it is, in my opinion, the way to conduct a political campaign in a democracy.

So I will try even harder, as a result of yesterday's primary, to state the Democratic principles as I understand them, to get the people's best judgment about America's problems and our prospects, and to help build a firmer peace, a truer prosperity and a fuller brotherhood for our nation.

In early April, I handed in my resignation to Roger Tubby. At first, he accepted it—then a day or so later, he made me a counter offer to stay on. I turned it down. In fact, I gave only one week's notice in order to leave as quickly as possible.

My plans didn't work out exactly as I had hoped. Somehow, Stevenson heard about what I had done and I received a phone call from his secretary that he wanted to see me. I dreaded going into his office. I knew he would think I was "abandoning ship" from a lost cause—yet, I also knew him well enough to realize that it would have been catastrophic had I explained how I felt about his campaign organization.

So we talked about how sorry I was to be leaving and how I wanted to return to the Southwest and all those trivial things that people discuss at a time like that to cover up deep feelings of distress and perhaps even resentment. His obvious disappointment in me hurt. In turn, I saw before me a tired and dispirited individual who seemed to expect more than I could deliver.

"I need to get back into the business of making a living," I told him lamely.

"Of course," he nodded. "I understand."

"I want you to know you'll always have my support," I said.

"Thank you," he said politely. "Where will you be going?"

"Oh, Oklahoma maybe—public relations in Tulsa or something like that."

"Oklahoma." He pronounced it like a foreign country.

"Or maybe Texas—I've always wanted to see what Texas is like."

I was beginning to feel more and more like a fool.

"I see," he said. "Of course. I understand."

But he didn't understand and I knew it. I left him sitting at his desk fumbling with some papers, looking very discouraged, and went on out.

Before leaving the city, I was tracked down by United Press for a comment to the effect that I was resigning because of my disapproval of the way the campaign was being run.

"No such thing," I said. "I'm just tired and I want to go home."

I did feel sick and it was a long time before I began to snap out of it. However much Stevenson guessed from that last conversation, I was never to know. But three months after my departure, I received a letter from Roger Tubby forwarded from my home address, telling me that "we are still undergoing a metamorphosis here and no doubt will continue to do so after the convention, assuming as I do that we will win."

Roger went on to say that Harry Ashmore had returned to the *Arkansas Gazette* and that two public relations chiefs had left and that "I probably ought to be making a reservation soon on the weekly train to Saranac Lake."

He concluded that "at least in the last two or three months you have missed some of the palpitation that has shaken the office."

The Minnesota upset was the turning point in the way Stevenson campaigned. From there on, he tried to "out-Kefauver" Kefauver. In Florida he swung through the state smiling, shaking hands, wearing funny hats, and behaving generally as he thought a practical politician should behave. He didn't change his speeches any but he did make an effort to be more folksy in a broad way.

185

In Oregon he won a write-in victory over Kefauver and then took the Florida primary from him by a slender margin. His efforts turned next to the June 5 primary in California with a prize of sixty-eight votes at the Democratic National Convention. He won it—but not without a tough, bitter battle with Kefauver.

In Dallas, where I was working in the advertising department of a jewelry store chain, I followed the rest of the campaign in the news. During the stormy convention in Chicago in August, I watched a few of the sessions, noted several familiar faces and felt glad that I had removed myself from the scene.

I was handling part-time assignments from the local INS bureau and at one point was sent to Love Field airport to join the other Dallas reporters in interviewing Stevenson's sister, Elizabeth Ives, who was on a campaign visit. I wondered how she would react at seeing me. I needn't have. She apparently had no recollection of ever having met me! And a short time later, I received a letter from her which had been forwarded to me—in which she addressed me at my old Chicago office number and pleasantly asked me to work up a biography on her for presentation to the press. I obligingly wrote it up for her, slipped it into an envelope and mailed it to her. Within a few days, back came a thank you—no offer to pay me for my time—just a nice little thank you.

On election night I watched the returns bury Stevenson in an avalanche of votes for the war hero. It was a complete rout. In the grand ballroom of Chicago's Conrad Hilton Hotel, where he had started his campaign officially a year earlier with his announcement, Stevenson read a telegram of concession, congratulated Eisenhower and pledged his support. Unlike his statement of concession four years earlier in Springfield, when the event held the glittering promise of a future try, there was a note of finality this time. Pointing out that there were things more valuable than victory at the polls, he thanked his supporters and then added:

"Let me add another thought for you who have traveled with me on this great journey:

"I have tried to chart the road to a new and better America. I want to say to all of you who have followed me that, while we have lost a battle, I am supremely confident that our cause will ultimately prevail, for America can only go forward. It cannot go backward or stand still.

"But even more urgent is the hope that our leaders will recognize that America wants to face up squarely to the facts of today's world. We don't want to draw back from them. We can't. We are ready for the test that we know history has set for us."

That night I wrote Stevenson—my first letter to him since that God-awful, hopeless day when I had left Chicago. Included in what I wrote him was a quote by author Irving Stone, in which someone had told Abraham Lincoln that he had had enough heartbreak to crush the average man, and had added—"but thank God, you are not the average man!" I also mentioned my ideas about mass communication trends in politics.

Back came Stevenson's reply:

January 2, 1957

My dear Pat:

I am mortified that I have not acknowledged your letter of November 13 long before this. The fact is that I didn't see it until this instant!

I should very much like to hear more about the mass communication propaganda; indeed we must know about it if we are going to cope with it in the future. I hope so much that some study of this kind can be undertaken by the Democratic powers that be, and I have already talked at length about it. I shall talk more about it in Washington this week-end. Do send me along what you have in mind.

And bless you, my dear friend, for those gracious words from Irving Stone about our Illinois friend.

Sincerely,

Adlai E. Stevenson

187

I did not send the material I had mentioned to him nor did I write him again about the campaign. It was too late for him and, as far as I was concerned, all over for me, too. The scars would be a long time healing.

*   *   *

During the eight years following, I married a newsman and settled down in Memphis, Tennessee, to raise our daughter—occasionally stumbling across a memento of the Stevenson years while unpacking the cardboard boxes which all news people use to store news clips and assorted photos. Sometimes I saw Stevenson on television and often I read about him, particularly after he became United States Ambassador to the United Nations. Always I felt that some day we would have a chance to get together again and talk things over and I would explain for the first time why I had walked out on him the way I did. It was a matter, I felt, which called for personal conversation, not the one-sided discourse of a letter.

But one day in 1965 I picked up the Memphis *Commercial Appeal* to discover that Stevenson had come through Memphis the day before on his way to address a meeting of Rotarians in Arkansas and had been interviewed at the airport. According to the news story, he had chain smoked. On impulse, I clipped out the photo and story, scribbled a kidding note on it and mailed it to him. Almost at once, he wrote me:

June 8, 1965

Dear Pat:

I didn't light one from another! I smoked one at most.

I didn't speak to 2,000 Rotarians—it was 1,200.

I didn't have on a double breasted suit—as the photo clearly shows.

And I didn't say "denomination"; I said dimension.

Otherwise it was reasonably accurate!

But what a joy to hear from you again. I wish we were in Springfield!

Yours,
Adlai

I had the letter in my purse—unanswered—when the news was flashed that Stevenson had dropped dead in London. The day was July 14 and he was sixty-five years old.

He died of a heart attack on streets not far from where he had once lived with his family during his young days of government service. His close friend, CBS commentator Eric Sevareid was in London at the time and had spent the preceding evening chatting with him. Sevareid's broadcast after Stevenson's death moved me to tears and I wrote him about it. In replying, Sevareid referred to his visits years earlier in Springfield when we had discussed Stevenson for a radio commentary:

"I had a wonderful time with him in that week. I suppose this wound will heal up, more or less, but it's going to take time. We won't see his like again for quite a while, if ever."

During the months immediately following Stevenson's death, there was a spate of articles and books and editorials—measuring him, sentimentalizing him, criticizing him, and almost all speculating as to whether or not Stevenson would have made a good president. The old "Hamlet" bit was revived and kicked around some more. Several writers seemed to delight in recasting Adlai as a nice aristocrat who was intelligent enough but really ineffectual.

Aristocrat he was, and certainly sometimes ineffectual. But the implication of some writers that he was too much of a gentleman to fight annoyed me. Compared to Dwight David Eisenhower, the life of Adlai Stevenson was a constant inner turmoil. He fought to overcome a childhood tragedy profound enough to shatter the average person. He suffered a broken marriage, election defeats, associates who betrayed him and acquaintances who used him. And he suffered too much at the hands of writers who stupidly felt that, because *they* couldn't see it on *their* terms, Stevenson wasn't fighting.

The enigma of the man was not that he was an enigma but that his integrity was the painfully molded and protected core of his being and something not to be tampered with or compromised or exploited by anybody—conservative and liberal alike. He was what he was.

But aside from whatever personal problems he faced, he could not possibly overcome the one overriding factor which inexorably tolled his defeat at the polls—timing. He tried. During his second presidential campaign particularly, he fought his heart out. The times just were not right. Americans, who want bold thinkers and doers during Great Depressions, revert to the status quo when the turbulence dies. The era of the fifties called for the bland formula of peace, prosperity and pap—not for a change or a challenge.

Adlai Stevenson came his time too soon and died too early—and we were the ones who lost—not he.

Index